Heads i ... hip

SCHOOL LEADERSHIP AND MANAGEMENT SERIES

Series Editors: Brent Davies and John West-Burnham

Other titles in the series:

Effective Learning in Schools
by Christopher Bowring-Carr and John West-Burnham

Effective School Leaders
by John MacBeath and Kate Myers

From Bursar to School Business Manager
Reengineering leadership for resource management
by Fergus O'Sullivan, Angela Thody and Elizabeth Wood

Leadership and Professional Development in Schools
How to promote techniques for effective professional learning
by John West-Burnham and Fergus O'Sullivan

Managing Learning for Achievement
Strategies for raising achievement through effective learning
Edited by Christopher Bowring-Carr and John West-Burnham

Managing Quality in Schools (2nd edition)
by John West-Burnham

Middle Management in Schools
How to harmonise managing and teaching for an effective school
by Sonia Blandford

Reengineering and Total Quality in Schools
Edited by Brent Davies and John West-Burnham

Resource Management in Schools
Effective and practical strategies for the self-managing school
by Sonia Blandford

Strategic Marketing for Schools
How to integrate marketing and strategic development for an effective school
by Brent Davies and Linda Ellison

Forthcoming title:

Information and Communication Technology in Schools
by Paul James

Heads in Partnership

Working with your governors for a successful school

■ ■ ■

JOAN SALLIS

Pearson
Education

PEARSON EDUCATION LIMITED

Head Office:
Edinburgh Gate
Harlow CM20 2JE
Tel: +44 (0)1279 623623
Fax: +44 (0)1279 431059

London Office:
128 Long Acre
London WC2E 9AN
Tel: +44 (0)20 7447 2000
Fax: +44 (0)20 7240 5771
Website: www.educationminds.com

First published in Great Britain in 2001

© Pearson Education Limited 2001

The right of Joan Sallis to be identified as author of this work has been asserted by her
in accordance with the Copyright, Designs and Patents Act 1988.

ISBN 0 273 65385 7

British Library Cataloguing in Publication Data
A CIP catalogue record for this book can be obtained from the British Library

10 9 8 7 6 5 4 3 2 1

Typeset by Pantek Arts Ltd, Maidstone, Kent
Printed and bound in Great Britain by Bell & Bain Ltd, Glasgow

The Publishers' policy is to use paper manufactured from sustainable forests.

About the Author

■   ■   ■

Joan Sallis. Twenty-five years ago Joan Sallis was appointed by the then Secretary of State for Education to represent parents on the Taylor Committee on school governance. Its recommendations became law, making school governing bodies more widely representative of the school community.

Now the best-known writer and speaker in the country on the development of effective governing bodies and their relationship with headteachers and senior managers in schools, Joan has worked with heads in well over a hundred LEAs, written a number of best-selling guides for governors and spoken to at least 20,000 governors at training sessions and conferences. But she is best known for her weekly 'agony column' for school governors in the *Times Educational Supplement*, which she has written every week for 12 years.

Joan was recently installed as an Honorary Fellow of the London University Institute of Education, one of four universities to honour her, and in 1996 was awarded the OBE 'for services to education'. She is proud to be a governor of her local comprehensive school. She writes with passion and conviction about the contribution which a good governing body can make to a school's success, but she is also perceptive about the delicate relationships which underpin its work.

In particular Joan is aware of the unprecedented pressures on headteachers today, and seeks to ease them. She writes simply and evocatively, revealing a deep understanding of schools and concern for all those who work in them, as well as for the children and families they serve.

Contents

■ ■ ■

Introduction
What this book seeks to achieve.
Support for heads as well as governors; heads' personal
leadership reflected in the development of the governing body; care
and repair for relationships; a practical agenda for Monday week.

Part Two
Building the Relationship with Governors

Part Three
Working Together for a Successful School

Introduction

■ ■ ■

What this book seeks to achieve

This book is about a relationship crucial to the success of a school. It is not a new relationship, having been part of the law of the land from the earliest days of state education, but other changes in the system have made it a more sensitive one. It is a relationship which in recent years has been for some head-teachers an enriching and supportive experience, while becoming for others a threat of career-shaking proportions. I will be brave enough to say that there is not so far much help available to heads and aspiring heads in managing it, and if I am proved wrong by developments after this book appears, I shall be very pleased. In the meantime I shall try to provide some practical guidance.

Difficult times for headteachers

Heads need support as well as governors

The training of school governors has advanced rapidly in range and sophistica-tion, and the better informed and more confident the school governor community has become, and the more aware of its responsibilities, the more dangerous the lack of comparable help for senior managers seems to be. I am not talking so much about the organised support provided by in-service courses and conferences, but of the quiet, no-big-deal-yet access to a friendly ear or even shoulder which often used to be available to so many before schools became self-managing institutions. In most local authorities this has become a memory, and heads often feel lonely with the new problems they perceive in the relation-ship with governors. These problems may not have reached the point where the head would contemplate seeking help from his or her professional association, but they are already enough to disturb sleep and lessen enthusiasm.

1

Better relationships

Good relationships need common ground

Relationships have always made the difference between a successful and an unsuccessful school. Even before the management of schools took on such a high profile in the mid-eighties, schools were webs of relationships woven around that basic relationship of teacher and learner and branching out into the more complex networks of a learning community. But among professionals common goals and a largely shared culture can be assumed. When stresses occur in the relationship with governors, neither party can retreat into familiar lines of authority; both parties have power of different kinds; and there may be little common vocabulary of words and ideas. Many heads feel that no easy assumptions can be made about the motivation of these mixed ability, mixed experience, partners. There is no doubt that many senior managers are suffering greater or lesser degrees of stress, and 3500 replies to a survey of members by the National Association of Head Teachers in early 2000 showed the relationship with governors as a contributory factor for some.

> I naturally hope to be able to lessen the stress. But I should not be satisfied unless I also helped to make the relationship between senior managers and governors a productive one. My ideal is a school where the governing body has confidently assumed its legal role, where its members are working in harmony with each other and the professional staff. Clear aims are shared by all, including the wider community of parents, pupils and neighbours. Management is sure-footed because it rests upon well-debated decisions to which all will be committed. Decisions are robust because they take into account from the beginning questions likely to be asked by the community served by the school. A strong and durable culture of continuing improvement reflects the wide range of interests committed to it.

Leadership may involve empowering governors

The chronicles of failing schools reflect the absence of all the qualities mentioned in the last paragraph. Above all they show the damage which can be caused by relationships without common purpose, trust or honour, qualities which are fundamental in a good team. As yet not all headteachers have fully realised how important their personal leadership can be in developing the governing body as an effective team – yet this is a service dedicated to the development of human beings. I do not suggest that heads should seek to control what should be an independent voice in school affairs, but by giving governors information, insight, confidence, and the ability to work more effectively together, they can strongly influence the *quality* of the governing body's contribution. Thus they may come to feel that situations in which previously they may have felt helpless are now ruled by reason: this can be very liberating.

'Care and repair' for relationships

Even where there is a will to co-operate, contacts between headteachers and governors are sometimes uneasy. Even where there is no hostility there may be no-one involved in the partnership who seems to know how to care for it and mend minor abrasions, how to make it a positive force to improve the quality of the environment, the relationships and the learning. The reasons for this vary widely and we shall look at some of the main forms of dysfunction in Chapter 4. We shall also look at expectations, clarify roles and boundaries, go in search of better recruitment and induction, and discuss more effective ways of thinking and working together for school improvement. But right now I want to say that I believe, from wide experience of what goes wrong, that *where there is the will* there is a 'nuts and bolts' solution.

A tool-kit for the asking

In my imaginary shed you will find, as well as nuts and bolts, lubricating oil to ease uncomfortable and clumsy relationships. You will find screws and nails and glue to mend things. You will find spanners to tighten up procedures, fuses to blow harmlessly when there is conflict, and circuit-breakers to protect relationships when difficult things have to be done. But do you have the motivation? That is the key to the shed. If no-one has given you the key, or it remains high up on a hook called professional pride, many little jobs neglected in the household of the school will become major malfunctions and sources of conflict and unhappiness. I can show you what is in the shed. I can show you where the key is. But only you can decide to pick it up and open the door.

Motivation is the key

You would expect a book of this kind to contain many practical ideas, but I do not know whether it can also change attitudes. I can point out that the legal role of the governing body is inescapable, with centuries of history and all political parties behind it, so that reluctance to accept it can only be a destructive force. I can point out the legitimacy of public supervision in a service where the individual school has acquired unprecedented autonomy, and the certainty that OFSTED will increasingly want evidence that that supervision is effective. I can demonstrate the opportunities to gain more public support for the values cherished by professional educators. I can sting professional pride by suggesting that good relationships with governors are a mark of the first-class headteacher. I attempt this in Chapter 1. But in the end I can only offer practical help to those who want it.

The other ten chapters in this book will thus consist mainly of practical help in managing the relationship with governors harmoniously and productively, backed up by checklists, models for helpful processes, and case studies to take readers a thoughtful distance from problems commonly experienced. In the four Appendices you will find summaries of current legislation, structures and regulations, and a brief history of public education to show how we got to this point and perhaps illuminate current issues.

An agenda for Monday week

You will not find many abstractions in this guide, few of those brave well-meaning words which give people a glow as they write them on flip charts at conferences and forget as soon as they get home, words like partnership, participation, consultation and communication. I often think the cleaners next morning couldn't guess the subject of the conference from the flip charts because they are all the same, and that it would be good if someone manufactured them ready written so we could go to the sea for the day instead. Nothing wrong with the words, but unless you decide what you are going to do on Monday week to make them real they will not in themselves move you on or keep you afloat in troubled waters. This guide is offered in the hope that it will help to turn fine words into practical Monday-week good practice – my challenge and yours.

Part One

▪ ▪ ▪

The Will to Make it Work

1
■ ■ ■
Why Should I?

> *It is understandable that headteachers don't find it easy to share authority with governing bodies and that some resent being accountable to non-professionals for decisions based as they see it, on professional expertise. I concede this in the chapter which follows. At the same time I am sure that to fight the law of the land which imposes that accountability is the road to personal stress and unhappiness and at extremes failure. It also bypasses many opportunities to excel. I hope to show in these pages that acceptance of the part the governing body plays in schools under current law is:*
>
> - *inescapable;*
> - *morally correct;*
> - *rewarding;*
> - *a mark of a first-class head.*

The new demands on headteachers

Heading up a school has never been a more demanding and potentially stressful job. A headteacher is no longer simply a lead professional, fitted by proven skills as an educational practitioner and experience of senior management to get the most out of other practitioners. He or she may have responsibility for a budget which can be as much as £3 million a year, for a considerable concentration of capital assets, for the safety and healthy development of up to 1500 young people, and for leading and managing a staff of as many as 150. That is by any standard a major managerial task.

In recent years this task has had to be performed against a background of rapidly changing law and regulations. The pressures on schools to raise standards and compete with each other has produced a much harsher environment than that in which most heads started their careers. The expectations of politicians and public have never been higher or the demands to achieve, to consult, and to respond to consumer demands stronger. The support available from the local authority has at the same time declined, and headteachers may often feel very lonely embarking on a much enlarged role for whose new elements they may have been only minimally prepared.

Heads and governors: not an easy relationship

The law clearly provides for this task to be shared with a governing body, a group of assorted local people nominated or elected by the school's providers (LEA or church), its parents and staff and its neighbours. You might think that a chance to share such a major responsibility would be welcomed by people under stress, but I have found in life that it's often just when the load of responsibility brings you near breaking point that you cling on to it for dear life, snatching from willing hands at every turn the cloth, the spreadsheet, the brush, the report, the saucepan, the baby.

The resistance and the resulting conflicts, then, are not unnatural. But they are destructive. I said in the Introduction to this book that there were nuts and bolts solutions to most of the problems heads encounter in working with governors, but you had to have the key to the shed where they were kept, i.e. the motivation. I must deal with that straight away, because it is fundamental.

Why should I?

Once at a conference a head made me angry. I hardly ever get angry although I believe you can always make something out of anger even if it's only a tea-cosy. All the heads were assembling in a fairly public hotel bar the evening before, and talking about what a rag-bag their governors were. This one said that hers knew nothing about the education system, nothing about her school, nothing about their role, and they never went to training or took any other steps to find out. 'It's not my job to see that they are well-informed' she said. 'Why should I?'

Why should I accept any responsibility for the development of my governing body? was the question. I answered with three more questions.

1   Who will if you don't?
2   Who'll suffer if you don't?
3   Who'll benefit if you do?

So at least I knew it was about motivation. I might have talked about expectations, which I'm going to do here in a while. But it was too big a subject for a hotel bar. I could also have asked why she felt comfortable saying her governors were hopeless in such a setting when she probably wouldn't say her staff were hopeless even to her bathroom mirror. That is a question I found and still find fascinating.

But the most useful thing I did was resolve privately that I would never again underrate the importance of motivation, or fail to answer the question 'Why should I?' even before it was asked. I offer four answers.

1. Good leadership includes the early recognition of the inevitable

Here to stay That isn't the best answer, indeed if the only reason for making a proper job of the relationship is that it's inescapable, it's pretty pathetic, but let's start with basics. There must be a few heads among those already close to shipwreck who haven't yet come to terms even with the fact that governors aren't going to go away. Not in the light of six hundred years of history, an important and increasing role for governing bodies in at least 13 major structural Education Acts and the support of all political parties (*see* Appendix I). Yet the actions of some heads can only be explained by a belief that if you keep quiet it will all vanish along with the Standard Attainment Tasks (SATs), the league tables, OFSTED, Education Action Zones, and all the other apparatus of governments seemingly at times obsessed with school failure. For if you are faced with a strong padlocked door you don't pick a quarrel with it, bruise your shins against it or pretend it isn't there, do you? Again, you think about keys.

Getting the messengers mixed up with the message It isn't hard, though, to see why so many do bruise their shins against the inevitable. What we experienced in the 1980s and early 1990s, and particularly in the Education Reform Act 1988, was the coming together of two quite separate historical processes, one respectable, ancient, and widely accepted, namely the belief in school-level lay supervision of professional activity, the other a Johnny-come-lately reverence for market forces as the best if not the only means of raising standards. The second was feared and disliked by many working in education. This must be what led so many heads to blame the messengers for messages they never wrote, to see in the new governors the agents of an alien philosophy which surely would go away if you waited long enough.

There would not have been a problem if the Taylor Report (*A New Partnership for our Schools*, HMSO 1977 – *see* Appendix I) had been implemented at once and without the unrelated aims which later got mixed up with it. There would then have been time to build our relationships before schools had to face so much change, and the new governors might have put obstructions in the way of the marketplace prophets or even scuttled the whole process of change. As things were, the marketplace philosophy had gained a strong hold before the reform of governing bodies was complete, and unrelated changes got linked in many important minds.

2. The legitimacy of the amateur

This, I would say, is something many education professionals find hard to accept. A common view, although not always openly expressed as such, seems to be that challenge to your opinions or actions is only acceptable if based on equal or greater expertise than your own. Indeed many teachers believe that they alone among experts, give or take perhaps the paper-hanger, are so plagued by interfering amateurs.

How teachers' perceptions must change Somehow the colleges where teachers learn their skills must go a bit further than a straight description of governors' responsibilities – which they are at least now required to do following Circular 10/97 – to the notion of lay trusteeship which is at the heart of all our institutions. Sadly, however, many of those who do the teaching gained their formative experience when that notion commanded little respect in schools. Meanwhile heads might try to help their own staff understand the concept, not only in the interests of better relationships in the school here and now, but also because those who may later rise to senior management posts will come adrift without such understanding.

I have been in many schools where the head is totally committed to governor involvement and yet the same old rubbish is still talked behind the staff-room door – 'I wouldn't try to tell my doctor/bank manager/plumber/mechanic ...' etc.

> *Do tell teachers that the Cabinet, MPs, and local councillors are all elected representatives of ordinary people, that magistrates and jurors are not lawyers, that every professional public service has its lay management authority, whatever it is called, making policy decisions, and that most non-executive directors of businesses have only the most general knowledge of the technicalities. These are the people who make the strategic policy decisions, though always with expert advice.*

The job of the professional experts, once they have advised, is to implement the agreed policies and almost every expert, in whatever field, is ultimately accountable to an authorised and in some sense representative lay body for his/her performance. At times in education this message has been blurred, especially after the Second World War when the country was fully occupied with rebuilding the education service. Public supervision then was at its least effective. (I return to this in more detail later in this chapter.) Teachers almost believed that control of the curriculum was theirs by right, when in fact this had never had any foundation in law or history.

Accountability in private transactions The facts hold even at the level of the individual client. No, of course you don't tell the plumber how to wipe a joint, or the best route from the tank to the tap, but you do tell him that what you want is hotter water for the bath, and he does discuss with you the fact that your bedroom floorboards will be up over the weekend, and that the pipes may make your bedroom a bit warm in summer. Then you meet and agree that the water to the bath is a lot hotter, thank you, and well, the bedroom will at least be very cosy in winter. You and the GP agree about what the problem is, he sets out the options if any, and you make an appointment later to review whether the treatment worked. You may have to sign a consent form if the treatment is surgery. You tell the garage in what circumstances you hear that funny noise, you tell the architect whether it's a sun-lounge or a laundry room, and of course you don't dream of telling them *how* to carry out your wishes.

> *Experts advise on what is possible, and experts carry out the work. But it is the client or the client's representative who has to* agree on the objectives, consent *to the methods, and* assess the outcome. *That is governance in a nutshell.*

Governors don't always respect the boundaries represented by those verbs highlighted above, but most sincerely want to understand them. Trespassing occurs in both directions, and if governors stray into inappropriate territory it is sometimes because they have not been allowed to assume their rightful role. My task – in Chapter 3 – is to clarify the respective roles and – throughout the book – offer both heads and governors practical ways of avoiding conflict.

3. Governors give strength to decisions and win acceptance for professional values

I probably don't even need to convince heads and governors that decisions made together are more robust, and that when school policies get buffeted and are in danger of being blown off course by the winds of ignorance or self-inter-est it is a lot better if they have been argued about before being firmly endorsed. 'Governors as ambassadors' is also a common theme, though it is rarely spelled out that the testimony of ordinary people who know the school can be worth tens of thousands spent on marketing.

Professional values are infectious I am thinking of something rather deeper than that, about how values cross frontiers, about how infectious certain pro-fessional attitudes can be. I sometimes wonder whether, if there hadn't been a change of government in 1997, there would have been some back-tracking on governors' powers, against the trends of history and logic, because too many had 'gone native', i.e. espoused some of the values professionals hold dear and thereby posed a threat to a more market-orientated service.

Take the issue of *child-centred primary education* and the broad curriculum r generally. The backlash against the extremes of the doctrine which pre in the 1960s was severe, and most people have no quarrel with a h continuity, progression and rigour in the curriculum and a readjustment in favour of basic skills. Yet I am fascinated by how many governors, including myself, have become worried about throwing out too many babies with the 1960s bath-water and about forgetting that it's beyond the paths that the flowers grow. I know many who have come to see that a narrowing of the curriculum can bring unacceptable inequalities to school life just as budget cuts have done, since the lucky homes fill the gaps and the rest go without. So a little scepticism has crept in about some of the extreme utilitarian attitudes, almost a reverence for the best life-enhancing teaching that governors have been privileged to see through close contact with their schools.

Again, take *special needs*. It is a small miracle that they have so soon become a priority with governors, indeed an obsession with some. It's spoilt my best joke, which is that the town I live in is the kind where a successful meeting on special needs would have to be called 'Are slow learners holding your child back?' That isn't true any more. You'd have standing room only whatever you called it and you'd be lucky if it didn't precipitate a demonstration. That is an extraordinary moral volte-face. Contact with schools and their values has convinced so many that achievers grow up in a world made up of other people's children, and that schools neglect any needs at society's peril. Since governors can so easily influence opinion outside the school gates we have here a very powerful check on extremes of all kinds, as well as an increasingly civilised influence in decision-making. But for this to happen governors must have opportunities to see the school at work and let the delicate interaction of teacher and child change them for ever. Their input into decisions must also be real.

I could go on. There's the support you get against *too much emphasis on competition* and on identifying failure. Governors aren't on the whole impressed by the idea of schools competing. The more they are encouraged into corner shop stances the more they cluster for mutual support. They see education as essentially a collaborative activity and too much competition as unnatural. Educators have always shared their ideas: they don't hide their work in the curve of their elbow like ten-year-olds doing a test. Then there's the excessive present-day concentration on identifying failure as a means of raising standards, excessive not so much in itself as in its share of activity, interest and resource. Experienced governors miss all the apparatus of helping schools and teachers through bad patches, identifying and spreading good practice, spotting the innovator and throwing a bit of extra resource that way. Lonely with their Action Plans, they wonder whether we aren't a bit too strong on diagnosis and a bit weak on cures. We like to know what's wrong but we *would* relish a bit of help in putting it right. Perhaps the clear responsibility of LEAs for raising standards set out in the School Standards and Framework Act 1998 will rectify this imbalance somewhat, but the attitudes of school governors could be very important.

4. A chance to shine

The final element in my four-pronged campaign for motivation appeals to professional pride. I believe that many heads miss an opportunity to become first class exemplars of their profession. As I begin this book, somewhat overwhelmed by the size of the task I have undertaken, and working almost every day to help governors through conflict and misunderstanding, I am the last person to underrate the magnitude of the challenge to headteachers which all the changes in law and practice demand.

> *Difficult above all for headteachers and governors is the business of managing an intrinsically problematic and sensitive relationship while coping with so much change in the job they have to do together. But the rewards are correspondingly great.*

I also believe that most headteachers want to excel, and I am convinced that before very long the relationship with governors will become the main determinant of excellence. Some good heads shy away from that extension paper, or don't turn up for the last exam, perhaps near the end of a fine career. I have felt so sad when more than a handful of heads taking early retirement tell me privately that it is because they cannot cope with the governor dimension. Yet the task is possible and the rewards immense.

Tomorrow's heads

What of those who aspire to headship? Increasingly those who select heads will be looking for the attitudes and skills which the relationship with governors demands, and candidates who have not become thoroughly familiar with the history and development of governing bodies, learnt the appropriate working rules, and developed some ideas of their own on how to build a partnership are unlikely to succeed. This makes it very desirable for present heads to share with senior staff in their schools what they are learning about the nuts and bolts of partnership. They also owe it to tomorrow's heads to set a good example.

Opening the door to higher standards

From now on I shall assume that all heads will wish to look critically at their own attitudes and keep the door open to do-it-better ideas. Worksheet 1.1 encourages senior managers at all levels to examine how they view governors. It is not intended to be too solemn, but it contains some typical attitudes and you might want to discuss with colleagues what – if anything – is wrong with these, which best describes your own present position and which you will aim at. Appendix I at the end of the book relates how we got to where we are. As far as I know there is no other brief guide to the milestones of state education to put the development of governing bodies in context.

> I hope I have shown understanding of the pressures under which today's heads are working. At the same time I have not disguised my fears for them and their schools if they turn those schools into a battleground. Learning cannot flourish in such an atmosphere. Decisions will lack conviction, actions will owe more to the need to preserve professional territory and amour propre than to raise standards, health and judgement will suffer from bruising one's shins against the inevitable. Above all, opportunities to make the school a strong united community in tune with its environment will be missed. Yet for those who have the motivation there are many simple, concrete measures that can be taken to build such a community, new ways of looking at old tensions, healthy processes, good habits and ways of working. Any headteacher with the will can manage better with governors. That is what this book tries to demonstrate. First let us look at the foundation of all relationships: expectations.

Worksheet 1.1:

■ ■ ■

How do you see your governors?

Governors do nothing but slow down the action. If I were honest I would have to say that I could run the school far better if they didn't exist.

It's a pretence. Governors are untrained amateurs, playing at being important. They don't represent anybody but themselves.

My parents are great and they help the school in every possible way. They don't need any formal committees to make their voices heard and I listen to them. The governors tend to be the stirrers.

I know you are going to say I sound like a Victorian wife but I suppose I'm quite lucky really – my governors don't bother me often! Once a term, keep it short, think of England.

My governors are so supportive – real ambassadors – and they all help in the school in practical ways. And the chairman provides a shoulder to lean on when I need it.

They mean well and they're good sorts. But out of their depth. They want me to take a lead and seem so relieved when I just advise them what to do.

The trouble is that so many have private agendas. I feel uneasy when I don't know where they are coming from. After all, would anybody do all that for love?

I'm really very fortunate. I have an accountant and a personnel officer on my governing body and they can take a lot of the difficult jobs.

It isn't often an easy partnership and sometimes my professional pride gets in the way. But I know that it is good for me to be challenged by people who represent my community. I respect them and they bring many fresh perspectives. Sometimes it saves me from too much haste, and decisions made together and through debate are stronger and more likely to be accepted. I feel safe when they are behind me.

Figure 1.1: How do you see your governors?

2
■ ■ ■

Great Expectations

This is perhaps the most important chapter in the book. It is the foundation of everything that follows. If we can leave Chapter 1 on the assumption that everyone wants to manage the head/governing body relationship better, we must now spend some time looking at:

- *what heads expect of their governing bodies;*
- *what the governing body expects of the head; and*
- *what governors expect of each other.*

I believe from my long experience of problems in the relationship that there is in nearly all schools a lack of clarity and rigour in mutual expectations which will in time result in conflict. If we can identify that and put it right we shall benefit fully from the practical guidance on working together which follows.

I shall first consider why we go wrong, then suggest that expectations need to be discussed in almost all relationships between heads and governors, and finally show in detail how appropriate expectations can lead to greater harmony and effectiveness in actually carrying out the work.

The part played by expectations

Expectations in relationships

All our relationships in life are built on expectations of each other. In work, in family life, in love and friendship, we have basic expectations which govern behaviour. Sometimes they are unspoken, often they have to be made explicit to move the relationship forward.

Most people would accept the following statements.

1 If expectations are not clear the result is confusion.
2 If they are too high they can lead to disappointment and conflict.
3 If they are too low they convey lack of respect and diminish efficiency.
4 When relationships are under stress, clear expectations provide stability.

In the early stages of a personal relationship, of rearing a family, going to a new school or job, expectations may have to be worked on for some time to make progress. Even when there is clarity there will be disappointments, but the expectations always provide a reference point for a fresh start. That reference point is vital between heads and governors, who so often feel slight unease with each other and don't know how to leave an awkward incident or hurt feeling behind.

Expectations in schools

Why are expectations of governors rarely mentioned? I spend much of my time now with teachers and heads, and I know that in their daily work the word expectations is always on their lips. They believe that the learning and behaviour of their pupils and the performance of staff whom they line-manage is founded on high expectations, which:

● clarify goals;
● increase self-esteem;
● improve performance;
● build confidence.

As in other relationships the expectations may have to be the subject of discussion, adjustment and explicit reminders. Most school rules are statements of expectations, so are home-school agreements, so are performance targets. Why is it then that the word expectations has never even been mentioned in any discussion I have had with educationists about the relationship with governors unless I have initiated it? Why is there so much evidence that the question has never been considered and that in many schools all parties are at a loss for ideas on how to improve the relationship and the working practices that go with it? It can't just be because most heads wish governing bodies would go away and never come back, and only think about them at all when they have to. Or can it? Surely, given that the governing body is a statutory body, no more 'voluntary' than a magistrates court, heads should expect from it the fairest, most responsible and thoughtful decisions.

The problem arises, I think, from confusion between the governing body with its serious role founded in law, and the individual governors, who are volunteers. If they were chosen by senior management for the job and paid an allowance – an appalling thought – there would be no problem about expectations.

Do volunteers need excuses?

Having accepted that only the highest expectations do justice to the legal standing of the governing body, maybe we must now look at how we view individual volunteers, and even turn some old concepts on their heads. Here too I think we must show rigour, and challenge the well-meant but misguided plea of many a headteacher: 'After all they are only volunteers.' It may be kindly meant, but in fact it diminishes governors. Nobody forced them to take on this serious and important job. They can leave when they like. That isn't a reason for making excuses for them, but rather a reason for having high expectations of them *and communicating them*. I don't just mean in words: heads with their natural skills and training know just how to convey expectations by raising an eyebrow, giving half a smile and taking it back, kicking a ball, not finishing a sentence, writing something on the back of an envelope, making assumptions. It is a trick of the trade. They may *choose* not to try those tricks on volunteers, with the most generous of motives.

But isn't there abundant evidence that governors lack encouragement to do their best? And by making excuses for volunteers, don't we devalue them and the whole idea of community service? Don't we harm schools by devaluing governors? Obviously volunteers need the stimulus of high expectations too, and the respect that underpins them, not just as individuals but in recognition of the vital job they do together.

High expectations all round

Headteachers should therefore stop making excuses for their governing body and show them the respect owed to a group of people doing a vital job. The same reasoning means that governors must have high expectations of head-teachers, the gatekeepers of the knowledge, information and access that the governing body needs to do the job well. It also means that governors have high expectations of each other, voluntary participants in a vital shared legal responsibility which they can only exercise together. What's more, they represent others in the education of their children, and have no right to take that responsibility lightly. True they have livings to earn and/or homes to run as well, so the processes they establish for turning expectations into activity must be realistic and efficient and their involvement genuinely strategic.

All this means not only changing our view of volunteering but also changing the tone of voice in which we refer to it. Not 'I suppose they *are* only volunteers', but 'For heaven's sake they're *volunteers*'. Not conscripts or slaves. That is why heads must expect individual governors to do their best and why governors in turn expect heads to support them as well as they can. And, while there may also be governors who use the 'volunteer' card to excuse low standards, most that I have met – and they are thousands – expect each other to be honest, eager to learn, hard-working team players, loyal to colleagues and the decisions made together, casting out personal interest and prejudice, willing to give and receive tough love to build a group culture based on these expectations, always putting the school first. I believe that this is the only route to better governance and the only way we have of putting the mutual respect we often idly claim to the test. Heads have high expectations of staff because they value them. They would not speak ill of them in a hotel bar, not only because they value them but because they know that staff quality reflects in part their expectations and their leadership. If we could look forward to a time when heads would feel just as inhibited, for the same reasons, in entering the kind of competition they go in for about who has the most awful governors, we should make real progress. Heads' contribution to the development of a good team would then be widely accepted as a measure of their skills as managers and leaders and they would be proud to show them off.

What high expectations mean in practice

I promised not to offer a set of flip-chart abstractions. Feelings and attitudes are important and I've spoken of them at length, but mainly because they result in high standards and good working practices.

1. How head teachers can bring out the best in the governing body

If heads have high expectations of their governors they will:

- do all they can to encourage the recruitment of committed people (*see* Chapter 5);
- contribute to an effective induction process (*see* Chapter 5);
- find out about the talents, life-skills and interests of their governors so that they can value them as people and build this knowledge into their expectations (*see* Worksheet 5.1);
- see the development of the team as something deserving their professional support – after all the school needs quality governance, and as leaders in a service devoted to the development of human beings heads should be proud to apply those skills to the governing body (*see* Chapter 7 and its worksheets);
- encourage the governing body to develop a culture in which the group itself sets standards of commitment, hard work, loyalty and mutual help, and gently but firmly communicate their own support for those standards (Chapter 7);
- take pride in the growth of an effective governing body as a measure of their own leadership skills.

Later on we look at some of these tasks in detail. Yes, heads are 'educating' governors in the best sense of the word, but without any hint of patronage or manipulation. The ultimate skill of the professional educator is to help people to think and act independently, and if the learners are adults and free to leave when they like, you have to be good at it. Returning for a moment to the 'why should I?' head, if her professional pride had ever played any part in the task of developing the governors' independent role, as it surely had in developing her staff's strengths and talents, she would have been ashamed to advertise her failure so lightheartedly for all to hear. My hope is that one day I shall hear heads gathering for a conference who boast about their governing bodies in the hotel bar and exchange good ideas for their development with their peers. Then I shall know that success in this relationship, like successful development of staff, is a matter for pride, seen by all as the mark of the first-class head.

2. How governors show their expectations of each other

Governing bodies demonstrate a culture of high expectation through the processes they establish for their own work as a team and their willingness to give and take tough love when an individual falls short. It means you don't have to be grateful just because Charlie did manage to write a scruffy piece on the subject he'd promised to research, even though it was late, full of inaccuracies, unfinished and into the bargain left at home. It does mean *noticing* when people don't turn up to a school event, and establishing report-back opportunities for important tasks. It does mean being a little more explicit than volunteer groups sometimes are about roles, work-sharing, rules and general behaviour. For instance:

- the governing body establishes clear arrangements for sharing the work, i.e. service on committees, participation in appointments, paperwork of all kinds;
- they aim at high standards of attendance and punctuality at meetings, not automatically accepting reasons for absence as adequate (they are now required to 'approve' absences, which underlines this point);
- they agree on a system for every governor to observe the school at work at regular intervals and make sure it is maintained;
- they have training on the agenda, expect every governor to take it seriously, and work to improve through the efforts of individuals the range of knowledge and skills available to the group;
- they ensure that all governors – including the head – know the working-together rules and aren't too ready to excuse mistakes;
- they accept that any governor who departs from agreed standards of work-sharing, is indiscreet, abuses corporate loyalty, or behaves otherwise inappropriately, deserves the disapproval of colleagues;

- they make it clear that all governors do their best to attend school events;
- they help each other, in particular encouraging members who find it hard to contribute and helping those who find their role difficult.

3. What governors expect of the headteacher

In working with governors and asking them what they expect of their head-teachers, I have found the most common statement by far was that they wished to be trusted and respected and not to have their motives looked at with suspicion. They were also very concerned that they should be told every-thing, good and bad, about the school. As for information, headteachers' conditions of service require them to supply the governing body with the information they need to carry out their duties, and there is a strong plea emerging from the governor community that they should be able to rely on the information being objective, putting all the professional arguments for and against each proposal before them with scrupulous fairness, that it should be concise, given the limits on governors' time, and that it should be in plain and living language without jargon.

The paper that emanates from a school, its volume, suitability and readability is a big subject tackled later (Chapter 9). Here I need say only that it's the source of a great deal of criticism. A point often made is that if they don't know what exists it's impossible for them to ask for it, and they have to trust heads to try to spread the options before them so that they can choose what they need. They also often haven't much idea of what information would be unreasonable to ask for and which could be extracted by pressing a button, so heads might well make suggestions as to what information, albeit not currently on tap, could be extracted fairly easily to help governors with particular tasks.

I shall be returning later to governors' information needs, but here I need only say that the commonest mistake governors make is to try to keep up with everything teachers know, think and do. Given that they have other lives to lead, this is as useless as trying to overtake the horse in front on a merry-go-round. Information given to governors which supports their strategic role without making them poor imitations of teachers needs to be rigorously selected; this requires a lot of skill. Often busy heads drown them in unse-lected written material because it's quicker.

A governing body which has no false modesty will also consider it reasonable that the head should help them understand as much as possible about the school, welcome them to see it at work, help them with team-building problems and trust them with even delicate information when necessary.

Field work

I shall not list here what I think would be reasonable expectations for governors to have of heads because I have such a good list contributed by governors themselves (*see* Worksheet 2.1). Over a decade or more I have developed a model of a day conference on expectations with groups of heads and governors working together. I have done this in Cumbria, Hampshire, Gwent, Northamptonshire, Leicestershire and Dorset, and hope soon to try it in one of the new urban unitary authorities. This is a day at which heads and governors talk without inhibition about their expectations of each other. The format had to be right, since it soon became clear that:

- it was no use having this discussion unless governors and heads were there together to share the learning;
- nevertheless, if you wanted frank answers, heads and governors had to be separated just for the first session to reveal their own expectations of the other partner;
- the composite product of that first session had to be shared with all participants; and
- heads and governors from the same school had to get together briefly at the end to discuss the outcomes with a view to improving their own practice. In short it produced corporate frankness without embarrassing individuals.

The composite version of the lists produced by heads and governors during those conferences is presented at Worksheet 2.1. I have tried to select the points which came up most frequently and were most central to the work of the governing body. It was noticeable that the governors' lists varied very little from conference to conference and were general and positive in their statements of what they most wanted. The heads' lists were much more varied and difficult to convert into a composite form. They included many points arising from particular individual experiences of a negative kind which were of limited general interest. In reporting these they naturally slipped easily into 'thou-shalt-not' language, and I hesitated to consign these to posterity, since I know that outbursts of momentary exasperation don't keep too well. The heads' list does, however, faithfully include all points which were raised at more than one conference.

These were excellent conferences and not too difficult to run. I thought there was a lot more useful work to do within that framework. At the very least, however, consider whether it would be useful to discuss these lists with your governing body, some of your colleagues, or fellow participants in NVQH or Headlamp courses.

Conclusion

I hope this chapter has argued convincingly that expectations are fundamental in any honest relationship, and that in the head/governing body relationship they hold the key to better understanding, mutual respect, and the pursuit of higher standards. I hope to have persuaded you that expectations need to be discussed, clarified, perhaps negotiated, and that the fact that individual governors are volunteers – while forming a body that has legal status and wide-ranging powers – doesn't excuse low expectations, but makes the case for high ones even stronger. Above all I hope that I have suggested how clarity about expectations can be used to promote better practices, procedures and quality in the work we do together.*

Worksheet 2.1:

■ ■ ■

Expectations of each other

These two pages arose from a series of conferences in different LEAS in which heads and governors debated their expectations of each other. You may like to discuss them with your governors.

Headteachers

We expect our governors to:

- respect the boundaries between governors' role in the formation of school policies and the day-by-day management of the school
- develop understanding of the school at work, reading all they can, spending time observing classes, and supporting our big events
- take a broad strategic view of the school's interests, setting aside purely short-term or sectional concerns
- work as a team, remembering that individual governors have no power to solve problems on their own, and avoiding factions
- share teachers' enthusiasm, value their achievements and show concern for their well-being
- remember that the school serves children of all abilities and to be equally concerned for those who find learning difficult
- develop working practices which encourage all governors to contribute and do their best
- be loyal to the school in their contacts with parents and community, and discreet about matters affecting individual teachers and children
- confine themselves to matters of school policy and encourage parents to bring purely individual concerns to the headteacher in the first instance
- appreciate the problems and stress associated with managing a school today, and be tolerant of those who have this responsibility.

Governors

We expect our headteacher to:

- respect and value us
- accept that in our different ways we are all there for the sake of the children, and not suspect our motives
- give us the information we need to carry out our role
- share everything with us, good and bad, and trust us to be discreet
- help us to see where we can intervene strategically to improve teaching and learning
- help us to become aware in advance of matters which require decisions, so that we are not always too late to make a difference
- encourage us to visit classes and help us build good relationships with all the staff
- explain the role of governors to teachers and try to ensure that they do not suspect or resent our interest
- help us with our teamwork, and especially help us operate on a basis of the equality of all governors
- understand that we have our livings to earn and our homes to look after, and select and simplify information so that we can use our time well
- speak and write in plain language without jargon
- accept that we mean well and that if we say the wrong thing it is usually just clumsiness or lack of the right words
- accept that if heads choose to become governors, they must be familiar with the rules of working together and must be loyal to decisions we all make.

3
■ ■ ■
Roles and Boundaries

Chapter 1 stresses that headteachers must accept governing bodies as part of the law of the land and here to stay, their role legitimate and supportive, a good relationship with them the mark of the first-class headteacher. Chapter 2 emphasises and illustrates the vital importance of explicit and appropriate expectations in this relationship, to achieve both clarity and high standards of work. But that leaves many heads still intensely concerned about professional territory, and how to protect it. Both heads and governors need to be clear about their role and its limits if they are to work together constructively. There is a steady muttering, occasionally reaching a high pitch, from headteachers about 'rogue governors', 'power-mad' governors, governors trying to take over the management of the school. Some of this may reflect resentment that we have governors at all, but I accept that a small number of governors do get it wrong from time to time and cause disproportionate trouble.

Heads often plead for more clarity about demarcation lines. This chapter examines the whole question of roles and boundaries, looks into recent history to show why in some schools these have become confused, offers some guidance on the interpretation of current responsibilities, with examples, and urges tolerance and flexibility in interpretation day by day. The guidance is so written as to be easily extractable for sharing with governors, and a separate set of guidelines (Worksheet 3.1) is appended for you to offer your governing body if you wish.

Where we came in

Are white lines ancient history?

Forty years ago it was common for schools to have white lines painted somewhere near the entrance to indicate how far parents could go without an appointment. Sometimes there was even a notice saying 'No parents beyond this point'. Nowadays in almost any primary school parents will be inside at the beginning and end of the day helping small children put on or take off their coats or wellington boots. They may take the opportunity to raise small problems with the teacher. There will be parents helping in classrooms in many schools of all types. In some they will even be helping to frame school rules or plan activities. It is true that Dunblane and other tragedies have made entry phones, reception rotas and visitors' badges into a modern white line, but schools pride themselves on making legitimate visitors welcome. Can we then say that white lines, security apart, have vanished into folklore?

Sadly, you would not think so if you had recently had a conversation with almost any governor or any headteacher. The governor would say there *are* still white lines and my goodness, don't you know if you have crossed them: they are just invisible now. As for headteachers, much of what they discuss at their conferences or in conversation with their peers, get their representatives to see Ministers about, or write to my TES Agenda column for guidance on, is in one way or another about territory. They refer to 'rogue governors' intent on causing mayhem. Many governors complain about heads who protect their territory unreasonably, and they too wish to be reassured that their legal role is recognised. They also want to convince heads that, while as governors they legitimately seek a clear area of influence for the governing body, they have no wish to run the school.

We need to ask whether the law and the rules indeed lack clarity or whether, in cases which lead to conflict, it is simply that one or other party wishes the rules were different. But first it may be helpful to ask why in the last decade territory has become such a major preoccupation.

Why is everybody so preoccupied with territory?

For the formative years of many headteachers now in post (say 1965 to 1980) school governing bodies were scarcely a source of fear or conflict. Yet as Appendix 1 relates, their centuries-old history provides glimpses of the essential part they played in schools of all types, and many quotations from Victorian debates about territory sound so modern that they could pass for campaigning cries from a governors' pressure-group in the 1990s.

But that potted history also relates that, while the three major Education Acts of 1870, 1902 and 1944 required governors to be appointed for every school and gave them an important-sounding role, none offered guidance as to who they should be, and all simply made local authorities (or the foundation in voluntary schools) responsible for choosing them. The system never tapped the immediacy and intensity of interest which parents, teachers and neighbours might have brought to the duty of vigilance. As time went on the method of selection came to be a dead hand on a potentially dynamic institution, especially as schools had little real independence in a managerial sense before 1988, and both LEA and, to a lesser extent, church foundation appointees could easily degenerate into mere site agents of the contractor.

The curriculum in all those years was the legal responsibility of the local authority. But the increasing diversity and sophistication of learning materials and methods made detailed control impracticable, teachers' unions exercised considerable power, and schools thus acquired in practice growing freedom within a prevailing culture of permissiveness. Few heads and teachers pined for managerial independence as long as teachers were able to express their ideas with little restraint in the classroom, so within a secure framework of LEA funding and administrative support, professionals enjoyed a freedom never before or since experienced, while governing bodies, whose method of selection and lack of role clarity have already been mentioned, declined in influence. In the 1960s and 1970s public influence over children's learning was weaker than at any time before or since. We are all familiar with the abuses of that freedom which brought a few schools to the headlines and provoked the cruel backlash of the Black Papers and everything they symbolised. We have all paid dearly for those excesses, especially, in my view, children in the early stages of schooling. Nevertheless, professionals must accept that public opinion – almost inevitably – was reacting against what many politicians, parents and members of the general public saw as a period of dangerous experimentation with a minimum of public control.

A sense of false security

Coming back to heads and the preoccupation of many of them with territory, this is understandable in those whose youthful years in the profession coincided with that carefree time. Typically they enjoyed, if that is the word:

- a high degree of independence in the classroom;
- a local authority ready to cope with everything that disturbed the peace, from a hopeless teacher to a broken window;
- a governing body which was mostly benevolent but whose level of intervention ranged from the superficial to the near-invisible;
- parents as far behind the white line as you chose to keep them.

Then, from 1979, with what seemed indecent haste, a new Conservative government first put parental choice and rights to information on what turned out to be a fairly wobbly pedestal, and then took the sole control of school governor selection away from local authorities and (to a much more limited extent) from voluntary bodies. They brought onto governing bodies people who, in the eyes of many heads, were eager and demanding parents, teacher activists and an alarmingly unpredictable importation from the local community. In no time at all the national curriculum, tests and league tables and OFSTED inspections were imposed on schools, which were simultaneously given control of budgets, appointments, discipline, and much besides. Schools were thus empowered because the government believed that local authorities, as well as teachers, had tolerated standards which were too low.

The new governing bodies

It must be emphasised that governing bodies had always had a clear strategic role, including legal responsibility for the general direction of the conduct and curriculum of the school, and were its trustees in every sense of the word. They still retained these sweeping responsibilities – among many more specific ones – after 1988, but the framework of the schooling system in which they exercised them had changed almost beyond recognition. The pressure on schools to compete, the rigours of the national curriculum, testing, published results, and the delegation of management to schools made these responsibilities suddenly much more serious. Besides, with the opening up of membership in 1986, many more governors now knew the school and cared personally about it, so responsibility for 'the conduct of the school' acquired more *real* content and force. But remember that governing bodies had also in this process been given, among other things, precise accountability to parents for the running of the school, the legal responsibility for planning the action to be taken in response to inspection reports, hiring and firing, control of the budget and of some especially sensitive curriculum areas like sex education and political education. You can't argue these powers away whatever you might think about them.

Small wonder that pride and fear soon combined to create an outbreak of territorial fervour which makes it hard work for people like me, week after week reminding all concerned of the legal requirements and the dangers of breaching them. It is even harder to demonstrate that it is potentially a source of strength for schools to have the awkward, sometimes challenging, but legitimate participation of ordinary people from the communities they serve, though I have many examples of that in practice.

I have acknowledged that these changes were a shock to those whose youth had been spent in the schools of the 1960s and 1970s, enjoying a level of professional freedom unknown in most professions, but most people outside education would say change had to come. I must also stress, however, that the legal powers of governing bodies are not new, merely defined with greater precision and detail, and given more weight by the influx of people more directly involved in the school and by the freeing of schools from local authority control.

Are the boundaries really obscure?

I've always thought the obscurity was greatly exaggerated. The intentions of the Education Acts 1986–1998 seem to me on the whole quite clear. But I accept that both heads and governing bodies are a long way from clarifying their respective roles in their day-by-day work, and that this is not only a danger to harmony and progress but could bring many schools close to shipwreck. I hope to convince heads that they can still influence the situation for good more than they ever thought possible. But they *must* accept the reality of the power-sharing represented by that legislation, which was carefully planned and democratically executed, and which has indeed if anything been strengthened by a government of another complexion. To pretend that only a bit of clarification stands between them and the almost unchallenged power they enjoyed *de facto* before 1986 not only flies in the face of the facts, but threatens the healthy development and accountability of their schools.

Guiding principles

Priority points for new governors

If I could have five minutes with new governors before their first meeting I know just what I would say. That is because I now know the most common causes of trouble.

Golden Rule 1. No power on your own

Firstly I would remind every new governor that you will not find anywhere in the law a statement of the role of the school governor. The individual has no power. Only the governing body, acting together by consensus or majority vote, within the rules, can change anything. Many governors don't really understand this. Nor does the occasional inexperienced head, who might even be frightened of the harm one difficult governor could do. If all partners realised what is involved in legally changing anything it would remove the fear and much of the difficult behaviour at a stroke. Even governors who do understand it forget it sometimes, when the desire to change something they see as the only fault in a beloved school, or the pressure of their interest group, becomes overwhelming. Only today before I wrote this I answered a sad letter from a keen, very new governor, who at the end of her first term of learning, listening, thinking, had written 'a few notes' for the head identifying some perceived weaknesses in the teaching and suggesting some timetable changes to make better use of staff strengths and some alterations in the management of breaks and lunch-times! Not surprisingly the head's response fell somewhat short of unqualified gratitude, and I had to tell her that she was wrong. But I'm sure she will be a good governor and deserves tolerance.

Golden Rule 2. Getting the level right

The second most common mistake is to fail to identify the proper level of governing body intervention, which is not of course the operational level. The most well-meaning governors may slip into 'checking-up' mode with little encouragement (actually breaking both golden rules). I must say somewhere, every week of my life, that a director of a shipping line does not punish a misbehaving crew member or check the lifebelts, but a good board of directors will identify the levers which affect crew motivation for the better, write guidelines on discipline, and see that there is a system on board for checking the lifebelts often enough to a suitable standard. I don't altogether like the board-of-directors analogy but this example seems to sink in (a) because the listener knows these directors couldn't drop in any time with a clip-board like an over-eager parent governor drops in to the equally deep water of a classroom and (b) because so many governing bodies exhaust themselves doing the dry-land equivalent of checking the lifebelts. They need to be told often that they are there to establish policies which ensure that these things are done, not to do them.

So where does the 'critical friend' come in?

The government and the governor training fraternity have become very fond of this phrase as a quick way of defining the governors' role, and it has caught on. It has now indeed been dignified by appearing in the Education (School Governors) (Terms of Reference) Regulations SI 2000/2122, which took effect on 1 September 2000. This worries me somewhat. I know what is intended by the phrase – we all recognise that someone who cares about you and wants you to look smart is entitled to tell you red doesn't suit you and that you ought to lose a bit of weight. But I hope people won't forget to say that the governing body, not the individual governor, is the critical friend. No school wants 20 critical friends, all with something different to say. I believe that headteachers expressed some concern about the phrase when the regulations were in draft, and I don't blame them, since out of context it could be encouraging individual governors to do just the sort of thing heads dislike most. It's also important to say that the critical element in the friendship isn't the product of a sudden good idea, but the result of a rather dull process of identifying a problem, considering various alternative strategic steps towards solving it, debating them within clear rules and coming to a conclusion. All together. What's more, as well as being corporate, the critical intervention must also be confined to matters which are the proper concern of the governing body. With all these conditions the phrase loses a lot of its natural glamour, but I don't like to think of 300,000 governors getting up every morning racking their brains for something both critical and friendly to say to the head!

Can we still talk about governance and management?

I have included as Appendix II a brief summary of the School Standards and Framework Act 1998, highlighting the role of governing bodies and the changes in the schooling system which will affect them. In the light of this I hope I can persuade you that the words 'governance' and 'management', so often used to justify protection of professional territory, cannot any longer be used to clarify boundaries. The Taylor Committee, which recommended the reforms of governing bodies implemented in 1986 (*see* Appendix I), had to decide whether to keep the term 'managers' (which used to be used in primary schools) or adopt the term 'governors' (as used in secondary schools) for both sectors. It could have gone either way, especially as management had little of the fashionable aura it enjoys today and 'manager' was little more than the masculine of manageress. One cannot believe it would have changed the course of history if they had plumped for 'managers' instead of 'governors', yet it would have made it impossible ever to claim that governors had no place in the management of schools.

We need better words than those to reflect what the law has prescribed and to bring clarity to our relationships. I think it is more accurate to say that the governing body constitutes the strategic level of school management while headteachers have the executive responsibility for the smooth day-by-day operation of the school, a responsibility which they should be able to exercise without constraint as long as they work within an agreed framework of policy. That in all conscience is a big enough job in present conditions and heads need all the friends they can get.

Are there no rogue governors?

Yes, of course there are. There are some governors who do not respect the boundaries just as there are heads who try to re-draw the lines to suit themselves, though the former seem to get more than their share of the headlines than my experience would warrant. I do not for one moment condone the actions of governors who might think they can direct teachers, interfere in the day-by-day disposition of time, space and human resource, challenge individual rewards and sanctions, but in the majority of cases they have not been well advised and act in innocence. I want governors to respect professional territory, and heads to accept that the governing body has a clear role backed by the law. But I wish we could be a little more forgiving about day-to-day mistakes and misunderstandings.

The meaning of 'strategic'

Some helpful illustrations

The words 'strategic' and 'operational' are not easy to understand in the abstract.

In the context of a school, however, it is perfectly clear that the headteacher alone is responsible for the following operational matters:

- deciding upon and implementing day by day, within agreed policies, the use of the resources of space, time, money, equipment and personnel available;
- maintaining and improving the quality of the teaching day by day;
- maintaining an orderly environment for learning, and responding on a day-by-day basis to any threat to that order from the actions of either teachers or pupils;
- giving such professional advice to the governing body as they may need or request to assist them in carrying out their duties;
- representing the school in day-by-day contact with the LEA, with parents, community agencies and other bodies impinging on the school.

The Statutory Instrument No 2000/2122 on Terms of Reference regulations referred to on page 31 sums this up in the phrase 'internal organisation, management and control of the school'. The list above is an attempt to put flesh on the bones of that definition and represents major responsibilities. I hope that it makes clear the kind of operational decisions which the governing body – and its individual members! – should leave alone altogether. The emphasis throughout is on 'day by day' because all responses to situations will be within a framework of agreed policy. A governing body which is working properly will already have influenced the quality of teaching, the availability of resources for particular purposes, and the responses to bad behaviour, through the many policies and processes in which it plays a part.

The list above may be shared with governors to help prevent them questioning who teaches which children where, whose lessons are boring, whose marking neglected, which punishments unfair. Such misconceptions of role often arise from innocent misunderstanding but they damage relationships.

How the governing body exercises strategic influence

In trying to clarify what governors do, the word 'strategic' often comes up. It occurs frequently in the Terms of Reference regulations already referred to (SI 2000/2122), and these regulations urge governors to delegate as many lesser functions as they can in order to have more time for their primary task of establishing a strategic framework for the school setting out its aims and objectives; the priorities and targets for achieving those aims and objectives; and the policies adopted to serve that end.

'Strategic' isn't an easy word to define except through examples. One can explain that the quality of teaching can be directly influenced by professionals on the spot through instruction, suggestion, example or reprimand, and less directly through the provision of suitable opportunities for observation or in-service training. Behaviour can be influenced through direct guidance, example, and suitable use of sanctions and rewards. But governors influence both teaching quality and behaviour through the senior appointments they make, through their wise use of the budget, through their efforts to provide a stimulating environment, through fair dealing in all matters – which raises both teacher and pupil morale – and through wise guidelines on discipline. Remember too that if a teacher or a pupil ever gets to the end of the road, the final word is with the governing body's discipline committee.

A governing body which understands 'strategic', confronted with evidence that performance in one particular subject area in the school is unsatisfactory, will not say 'Sack the head of that subject and send all the teachers on a course'. That is a process requiring a hammer in the school tool-box, whereas they are looking for levers. A lever is a strategic implement – a hammer a bit more operational! So they may consider the exam board they have chosen, if appropriate, and the syllabus. They may look at the size of the groups and their ability mix. Above all they may look at how they appoint middle managers. Take two days over it or one? Two governors involved or one? Set management-type questions, an in-tray exercise? They will also think about the job descriptions of these curriculum leaders and the non-contact time they give them to monitor teaching, update themselves in their subjects, acquaint themselves with new resources, and so on. They may look at attendance records and find how much of the under-performance was simply due to students who didn't actually turn up for the test or exam. Alternatively the governing body might, with the head's support, decide to buy in a consultant. The point to make is that the governing body are looking at ways in which they can change the conditions in which teachers teach, and this may involve a whole range of strategic levers. It is a professional's job to find face-to-face methods of making them teach better.

Grey areas – borderline between operational decisions and community concerns

There is a great deal of talk about grey areas, but in practice I have found that they nearly all amount to operational decisions which *also* have strong repercussions in home or community. They are, therefore, on the border between management of resources day by day and the governing body's responsibility to parents and neighbourhood.

Examples The best examples of this arise around pupil grouping, where changes disturb parents very much. If, for instance, a primary school has a problem which some degree of vertical grouping would solve (very common now as a way of reducing infant class sizes when you don't have an extra space or an extra teacher) the head might well argue that this was 'use of space and personnel' and therefore operational management. So it is, but because parents hate any messing around with children's groupings it would be a wise head who not only discussed it with the governing body beforehand to gain their support but sought their help to present it. Similarly with ability groupings in secondary schools. Reading policy is also a very sensitive area. Yes, everyone should accept that teachers best understand the different methods of teaching a child to read, but reading is so fundamental to progress, and the familiar texts often so dear to parents, that any major change might be better managed with the governing body's willing support.

> *With goodwill, these borderline cases can usually be resolved by a head who is prepared to explain and consult in good time about how changes can best be presented and implemented.*

Exclusions

A moving target I wish it were possible to avoid writing about exclusions at all, mainly because we have just been through a period when the government keeps changing its mind, and the words may be out of date as soon as they are written; also, I confess, because it is a painful issue in the roles and boundaries department. As a governor I dread having to do my turn on a hearing, because I know that, should we ever have to overturn the head's decision, we could jeopardise in a day the relationship we have worked so hard to build with head and staff, so fraught is the subject with emotion and pride. In both senses a moving target.

The process Only the head can make the decision to exclude (and he/she should never implicate the chair or any other governor). Then, if it is an exclusion to which such procedures apply, the governing body's statutory committee of three have a judicial role. They decide whether the head acted appropriately in all the circumstances and they have the power to order the reinstatement of the pupil. The LEA no longer has to confirm or reverse the decision and the next stage, if the parents appeal, is an independent committee with no connection to the school. If such a committee eventually decided in favour of the appellant it would probably be the worst possible outcome for the school, harder to bear I would guess than an immediate reversal by the governing body. I know that many governors have this in mind every step of the way, and for this reason, as well as for its own sake, take immense care to satisfy themselves that the school's case is rock-solid, the evidence factual and objective, presented without supposition or prejudice, the record of other strategies adopted convincing, the contact with parents beyond reproach.

Rescue operation If the worst were to happen, I hope heads and teachers would realise how hard a decision this is for governors. They are torn always between loyalty to the head and staff, a loyalty sharpened by their duty to other pupils in the school, and a solemn duty to be fair to the individual. Other pupils' education, safety and happiness have been threatened by the misdeeds of the pupil concerned. Against that an individual's school education will, on the best assumptions, have suffered a serious setback and on the worst may in effect have been terminated. The general parent body and the community can be assumed to come down on the side of the majority, and governors know this, which makes it doubly hard if they ever have doubts about the strength of the case against the excluded pupil. Whatever the outcome please believe that they have done their best.

An interesting practice In our school the head and staff have always invited a governor to the final review meeting before a permanent exclusion. I had nothing to do with the introduction of this practice and at times I have asked myself whether it's in harmony with the law, but everybody seems to be in favour of it and I don't think it's forbidden anywhere. It doesn't happen that often, so there's no formal rota except that the governor of the month will be asked first if eligible; otherwise, like most things, it depends on availability. It goes without saying that the governor who has done this will neither be on the panel of three if the exclusion takes place nor speak to the panel members about it, and that that governor expresses no opinion about the merits of the case or comes down on either side. The purpose is solely to provide an independent check on the process, the acceptability of the evidence, the efforts made to involve the parents and appropriate agencies, and the strategies tried to improve the pupils behaviour up to this point. The staff certainly like the practice, it has sometimes been constructive, and I cannot see that it in any way compromises the governing body's role.

How can roles be further clarified?

I really think we shall soon have to accept that at least basic induction training on roles, relationships and rules should be obligatory for governors. There should be much, much more about the governing body's role in courses for heads and aspiring heads and indeed in teachers' initial training, though from now on we should see some improvement in the last as a result of Circular 10/97. After all, if heads and teachers know the boundaries it's a start: often I find that complaints from heads about governors overstepping the mark are based on misinformation, wishful thinking or how things used to be, rather than on fact. And misinformation is the easiest to cure.

As for knowledge of the working-together rules, which I return to in Chapter 7, I am shocked by the prevailing casualness of both heads and governors in many cases about the simple statutory rules and procedures, which can be learnt in an hour and on which so much effectiveness, fairness and protection against dirty tricks depend. Unless we are going to return to a full clerking service, which in LEA schools in the old days was more often than not provided by a well-informed officer who would ensure that everything was done properly – and on the whole that system seems unlikely to return – heads and teachers really must take it seriously, for their own protection if nothing else. I wish I were free to recount all the experiences I have had through my agony column for governors of miscarriages of justice and really dirty tricks I may have just managed to prevent in time (and I'd sooner not think about the ones I don't see) which have been possible because some clever individual has taken advantage of others' unfamiliarity with the rules. You know how it is. You sit there thinking: 'That doesn't feel right to me, but I don't know where it says, and I don't want to look silly, so I'll say nothing.' So bad things happen.

LEAs vary a great deal in the support they wish to and are able to give to governing bodies. Some still behave in a more interventionist fashion than the law strictly supports, a few carry detachment to extremes, with many variations in between. I personally regret that LEAs on the whole don't seem to think that it is their job to mediate when heads and governing bodies get locked in disagreement. Realistically there is no-one else to do so. After all, they are still employers of the head in community schools, and the governing body is (at least at the time of writing!) answerable to them for the use of delegated funds and their role in the local service of education. Often the local governor training team are extremely helpful, but they vary enormously from LEA to LEA in the resourcing and status they enjoy, and sometimes find it hard to stand up to people they see as powerful.

School level whole-governing-body training and team-building are becoming more available and, because in the end individuals have to work with the colleagues they get, are an essential supplement to off-site training. Any attempt by the participants themselves to define boundaries could so easily become a power struggle.

I append to this chapter, as Worksheet 3.1, a basic guide to roles and boundaries which you might like to give to your governors. It should help a great deal in day-by-day relationships. In addition Appendix II (page 160) summarises the relevant parts of the 1998 Act and Appendix IV (page 167) the working-together rules made under it.

A plea for forbearance

This is a new relationship. All participants are learning on their feet and there are bound to be uneasy moments as they grow to respect roles and work together for common causes. Both headteachers and governing bodies will infringe boundaries from time to time, and the odd clumsy mistake of an individual governor or the territorial defensiveness of a head shouldn't be taken too dramatically by either. They all in the end should want the best for the school. The governing body's role has without doubt become more challenging to traditional patterns of school authority, not so much in itself as in the context of government policy for schools within which governors now operate. The independence which schools have under local management brings daunting responsibilities. The pressure to maintain and raise standards is intense, and the penalties for failure are cruel. In comparison with the governors of former days some of the new participants may be less smooth, less experienced, less detached, more intense and emotional in their concern. They too know that the decisions schools now have to make on their own are big decisions, sensitive decisions and, if you get them wrong, very conspicuous decisions. Many governors, especially chairs, work hard. Many heads are very tired. But all want the same things for the school in the end, even if they differ about the way to get there. Common aims always make it easier to be tolerant and forgiving, and salvaged pride is a poor substitute for most of the things we forfeit to protect it.

Note Throughout the book, but especially in this chapter, I have been concerned to emphasise the corporate nature of the governing body's powers, which has meant, perhaps tediously, using the words 'governing body' wherever the context is decision-making. If I have anywhere lapsed and used the word 'governors' too loosely, please take it that I do always mean to stress that individuals have no power to make decisions.

Worksheet 3.1:

■ ■ ■

Head's job or ours? A guide for governors

1 The boundary between the work of governors and that of the head and professional staff of the school is probably the subject that bothers both parties more than any other.

2 Individual governors often get into hot water for getting involved in what teachers see as the professional skills of teaching and senior managers see as the day-by-day running of the school. The first thing to say about that of course is that *individual* governors should be very careful what they get involved in at all because as individuals they have no *formal* role except to:

- contribute to the governing body's knowledge and understanding of the school at work;
- take part in its discussions of matters for which it is corporately responsible; and
- share in decisions it makes about those matters.

In other words it is the governing body which raises issues, questions policies and may eventually bring about change.

3 This does not mean that the individual governor cannot be a friendly, never threatening, presence round the school, a sharer of teachers' enthusiasms or frustrations, a visitor keen to learn more about the educational process and the way the school is organised, and an observer who will day by day quietly collect a great deal of experience and insight to bring to the work of the governing body. What the individual governor must remember, however, is that most of us have not been trained to teach, and even if we have, it doesn't give us any jurisdiction over teachers in that school. Nor have we been trained to manage a school, much less to inspect those who do.

4   Governors are often troubled about their responsibility for the curriculum. Governors as representatives of the public have been responsible for *what* schools teach for centuries, but the 'what' isn't the same as the 'how'. The governing body, with professional advice, would, for instance, have to approve the decision to start offering French in a primary school, change the second foreign language in a secondary school from German to Spanish, drop statistics or introduce rural studies. The governing body might be concerned if the school didn't teach fractions or spelling or citizenship – especially as they form part of the national curriculum. But *how* to teach fractions is a professional matter, and so is inspecting the teaching of fractions.

5   Perhaps the best next step is to look at what the headteacher, supported by his or her staff, does in the school. Legal regulations spell it out as 'responsibility for the internal organisation, management and control of the school'. In more detail, the headteacher:

- decides on the use of resources – time, space, staff, money, equipment – in the school day by day;
- ensures that the teaching is good and seeks always to improve it;
- maintains an ordered environment in which learning can take place, and deals on a day-to-day basis with anything which disturbs that order;
- communicates on the school's behalf with the LEA, parents and community, and other agencies concerned with children and young people;
- is governors' chief professional adviser, obliged to give them the information they need to carry out their role, and accountable to them for the efficient management of the school and the quality of teaching and learning.

6   Headteachers carry out all these functions within a framework of policies adopted by their governing bodies, and while they do so they are entitled to freedom from day-by-day interference in their work. Teachers are responsible to their headteacher for their actions and the quality of their teaching. Governors operate at the strategic level to support and advance the work of the school.

7   So we don't check up on the teaching or the finance officer's adding up. We don't question the detention given by a teacher to a cheeky child. We don't suggest that Miss Jones goes on a course or that Mr Black would be better with Year 6 than Year 2. We don't bring concerns to the school about every parent who thinks her child should be on a higher reading book or whose genius son is bored in maths. But what do we mean by a framework of policies? And what exactly is the 'strategic level'?

8 *Governing bodies exist to raise school standards long term by establishing clear aims, sound policies and effective systems of monitoring and accountability. The aim is a school which both protects and challenges; which is stimulating, efficient and fair; which breeds both individuality and community spirit; which is self-critical and aims at continuing improvement; which is a good employer and a good neighbour.*

9 How do we set about this? Well, every responsibility we have contributes. We try to spend the money wisely. We appoint good staff. We try to provide a physical environment which is safe, healthy, stimulating. In our personnel role we try to make good decisions about people, decisions based on fairness and open, consistent principles, and we ensure that in-service training has high priority. We establish sound guidelines to underpin the school's disciplinary processes. We help to shape the school's values and try to carry them into our development planning, policy-making and budgeting. All this helps to provide a strong framework for learning.

10 What about the business of raising standards? How can we get hold of this particular hot potato? Well, we need to be sure first of all that we have the right strategic information about performance flowing regularly our way, information which covers the whole ability range from the very gifted to those with statements of special educational needs, and also the entire activity of the school, clubs as well as exam results. We also need to be certain we have the fairest methods of judging our own results in the light of the abilities and attainments of the children when they join our school.

11 But what tools do we use to raise performance? How can we as governors make a difference specifically, not just through good appointments and a well-maintained building? You had the right word there – tools. One of the things we must learn is the range of other strategies which affect learning quality. A hammer is a good tool, but it is not a strategic tool. Using a hammer is like sending people on courses, reprimanding them, showing them how to do it better. It uses the strength of your arm and it operates where the problem is. A lever is better. It can affect things some way off and wield more strength than your arm. A lever is a strategic tool. What are the levers in a school? Some obvious ones are size of classes, ability mix of groups, syllabus or exam board. Less obvious are how you choose and use middle management, what sort of non-contact time curriculum leaders and departmental heads have to monitor and support the teaching of others, pay policy, the occasional use of consultancy. These give a school wide scope for interventions that affect performance, and keen detective work sometimes. They don't involve any interference in the classroom, yet they can have a real effect on teaching by making the framework more supportive and the monitoring more effective.

THE WILL TO MAKE IT WORK

12 *What it all amounts to is getting the level right, the level appropriate for people who have their living to earn, perhaps homes to run as well. You can't keep up with everything teachers think and do. If you were directors of a shipping line, you wouldn't order the crew about. You wouldn't decide what punishment to give a sailor found drunk on watch. You wouldn't fuel the boilers or check the lifebelts. Yet governors often waste a lot of time doing the dry-land equivalent of checking lifebelts. You'd take an interest in crew morale and the factors which affected it. You'd establish guidelines for discipline on board. You'd know how much fuel the ship used on a voyage. You'd make sure there was a system in place for checking the lifebelts carefully and regularly. And the captain would be accountable to you for managing the ship.*

13 If governors can get these demarcation lines clear in their minds there will be several good outcomes. Firstly their workload will be more manageable – if part-timers who are not professionals try to keep up with all the activity of full-time teachers it will be like trying to catch the horse in front of you on the roundabout. Secondly relationships will improve: teachers will be more at ease with you. Finally and most important, the job will be satisfying because you have found some of the secrets of school improvement. It's frustrating identifying things that could be improved and then realising that you don't have the power to intervene, and you will be able to see how, by helping to change the framework within which children are taught, you have actually improved their learning.

Part Two

■ ■ ■

Building the Relationship
with Governors

4
■ ■ ■

Common Problems and How to Solve Them

The law and regulations on governing bodies, looked at as a whole, aim to create a group of individuals who:

- *are equal in status and working as one*
- *operate at a strategic level*
- *take seriously the power they share*
- *have common aims*
- *are clear about roles and boundaries*
- *are honourable in their dealings, eschewing self-interest and prejudice.*

You may ask how such high-sounding aims can be extracted from a dry catalogue of rules and procedures. I can justify every one and give a reference to the section, sub-section or regulation in which the attribute is enshrined. When a governing body gets into difficulties it is usually because it has lost sight of one of those aims. Headteachers do worry about these situations, though they may often feel that there is nothing they personally can do about them. This chapter looks at the most common problems governing bodies experience, concentrating on how headteachers themselves may be able to help.

Should headteachers be governors of their schools?

This may on the face of it seem a strange question to put first in a chapter about how governing bodies go wrong. But when I began to think about these common problems I realised fully for the first time how much a headteacher could do to solve them, and indeed if I can't demonstrate that, and give some guidance, there isn't much point in identifying them here. But I would have to add 'provided the head is a governor' on every page, so I have to face that very difficult issue now. I don't know exactly how many heads have opted not to be governors, except that it is a minority.

The choice heads make

Ever since the major reform of governing bodies in 1986 headteachers have had the chance to opt out of being governors of their schools, though they retain the right to attend meetings of the governing body. In the latest restructuring in 1998 the government came close to removing that choice and saying that headteachers should automatically be members of their governing bodies, but before the final version saw the light of day some pressure had clearly been put on them to restore the choice, and that is how it stands.

Why do some heads opt out? I don't know personally any heads who have opted out of governorship, but I have met some at conferences and they often ask me what I think about their decision. They tell me that they feel they have more status and independence as professional advisers. They sometimes add that they fear being outvoted on an important matter and having to implement a decision they have openly disagreed with. My answer is that a head is and always will be chief professional adviser, so being part of the decision-making process as well is a bonus. As for the possibility of being outvoted, it's a serious matter being isolated in making a decision about something important whether or not you are a governor, and if you are a governor at least you can fight your corner without constraint.

Is there a downside?

These heads – the ones who have opted out of being governors – often seem to be uneasy about the last bit of that answer, as though they recognise the implication that there is a clear downside to not being a member of the governing body, more than the little matter, as they see it, of not having a vote. They had assumed, in fact, given that they could always attend meetings, that they could have their cake and eat it. If this is so, I think the government should have made the nature of the choice much clearer, and, while they were at it, also made explicit the duty of the head who did choose membership to observe corporate loyalty to the governing body and its decisions.

I see no logic or purpose in offering the choice at all and was very disappointed when in the latest round of changes the chance to remove it was missed. By the law of the land the governing body makes the major decisions about the school. What sort of head doesn't want to play a part in debating and making those decisions about his or her own school? Strictly speaking a non-governor head should confine any contributions to meetings to matters of fact and professional practice, a role which a liberal-minded governing body is normally happy to bestow even on a regular observer such as a deputy or on a co-opted member of a committee. But it would not be proper for a non-governor to play an active part in decisions where there is more than one point of view. I doubt whether those who opt out have fully taken that on board. Whatever their views about governors, they surely don't knowingly choose such low status in a process they can't escape? The chief executive in a business is normally a member of the board, as well as being senior professional adviser.

How other governors react to your choice

Few governors will have given it any thought, I guess, unless they have a new head who makes a different choice from the out-going one, or some specific happening makes it an issue. But I suspect that if asked directly most would like their head to be a member. I know that as a governor I am very glad that the headteacher is a member, and I would assume that a head who chose not to be was trying to keep his/her distance from the whole process. I would suspect that he/she didn't approve of governors. I might even wonder if opting out was an expression of distaste so strong that the aim was to undermine the governing body by withholding information and advice and by occasional strategic non-attendance, hoping thereby to render it ineffective. A dangerous game, given governors' legal powers and responsibilities. I don't think many would go that far, but perhaps all candidates for headship should at least be asked their views on this important matter at interview.

The influence which is at stake

In this chapter I am concerned to show how a skilled headteacher-governor can contribute to wise decisions, good relationships, and a strong team spirit, and many examples follow. A decision not to be a governor inevitably diminishes those opportunities.

Common features of schools in trouble

One of the most depressing, yet in its way illuminating, experiences I have had was reading hot off the press five years or so ago the report on that junior school in Nottingham where the teachers refused to teach an excluded pupil reinstated by governors, and where that provoked a period of closure and an official enquiry. I was whisked back in memory to 1976 and the official report on the William Tyndale schools, duty reading for me as a member of the Taylor Committee which was then halfway through its work. I had been innocent enough to think that that dispute was about long-haired teachers and let-it-all-hang-out primary teaching methods, as described in the popular press. But reading the report I realised that, stripped of its local habitation and superficial characteristics, it was in its essentials no more about primary teaching methods than the Nottingham report was about a dispute over an exclusion. Almost all the reports I have read on school crises – and OFSTED may have made this a commonplace – are about the same things

When a school is on the skids you are most likely to find at least one of these elements present among the causes identified:

- confusion about roles;
- no sense of corporate responsibility: powerful individuals or small groups trying to solve things on their own, private agendas, A and B teams, disloyalty;
- absence of clear shared aims;
- poor communication;
- weak leadership.

Leadership quality may be preordained in your stars or your DNA, but those who can put the other things on the list right have gone some way towards proving they have it.

Communication deserves its own space and will be covered in Chapter 8. The other elements, namely:

- getting roles and boundaries right;
- working together as a team;
- equal status for all governors;
- working to clear common aims;

should surely be the cornerstones of governor training, governing body procedures, and relationships between governors and professionals, and I shall concentrate on them in this chapter. In the hundreds of governor problems which come my way every year these are recurring themes, and when a governing body is failing in even one of these respects it endangers the school. A headteacher may not feel able to tackle problems overtly, but I think you will be surprised how much influence you can have as soon you see the basic problem clearly.

> *The rest of this chapter is about using your influence as a headteacher-governor to help solve common problems. It covers getting the roles right, achieving equality of status for all members and establishing clear common aims.*

1. Roles

This section covers getting the level right, responding to parent concerns, preventing typecasting, and keeping governors ahead of the action.

Getting the level right

Inexperienced governors often start in checking-up mode. This has already occupied much space (Chapter 3), but it cannot be said too often that governors must understand fully the *appropriate* level for their intervention. If they do, we shall hear no more stories about parent-governor Penny coming in with a notebook on her first Monday morning and making notes on that hopeless teacher the parents are all talking about at the gate. We shall have no heads screaming about Penny's friend Megan who tries to use governors' meetings to report a long list of supermarket conversations about injustices to individual children. I shall see no more furrowed brows as Ken checks the columns of figures already checked by paid staff. As for Barbara, a tutor at the teacher-training establishment now part of the university, she'll be a great governor if you can only keep her out of day-by-day classroom management and put her good brain, along with others, to some of your real organisational problems.

> *Your role as head is not to react directly to inappropriate actions – it is the chair's job to do that – but to make sure that in your relationship with the governing body you always acknowledge their right to intervene appropriately and sometimes even help them to do so.*

Encouraging your governors to 'think strategic'

This will take time, and it isn't easy. Many schools drift into appallingly bad relationships and worse because their heads either react confrontationally or suffer in tight-lipped silence what they see as 'meddling' and never as much as try a positive response. But if you can accept that most governors involve themselves at the operational level because they aren't sure how else to tackle a problem, it is the only hope – and you must of course then stand by your word and welcome discussion of strategic options.

Many governors have very limited knowledge of how, for instance, a school approaches issues of teacher quality: the parents who pester governors to 'do something' know even less. You can't share with either the problem of an individual teacher, and you must make this and the reasons for it clear. But you can, at a quiet time when there is no such problem, make sure that all parties know the many ways in which the school maintains quality and gives support to any staff who need it.

Interest governors in the systems, not the application

Similar tactics apply to the school's systems for monitoring and checking other things that go on in the school – accounts, truancy, drugs, losses of personal property or school equipment. Governors are entitled to ask questions about these systems and even suggest improvements. Often all they want is to be told that whatever the problem, someone knows it exists, and someone has a system for dealing with it. But your explanations must also accept the possibility that they might want to comment on that system or even seek to improve it. *That is their right in law.*

Responding to parent concerns

An essential part of getting roles right involves helping governors – especially parent-governors who find it difficult – to handle the concerns individual parents bring to them. I hope that if you are lucky enough to have an in-school team-building session from your LEA governor training team they will stress that the governing body is concerned with policy and is not a complaints committee. Parent-governors do sometimes need to be reminded that, while they are entitled to ask for any general matter of parent concern, or any widespread criticism of a school policy, to be put on the agenda, they must encourage those with purely individual worries to take them directly to the teacher or head. But you as headteacher can do so many things.

1   You can first make sure that your school really is as welcoming to parents with concerns as it thinks it is: a well-publicised weekly half-hour session when a member of staff will always be there to hear individual worries, however small, is good practice. It builds confidence in you, it ensures that the school is well-informed about parents' concerns, and it takes the pressure off governors.

2   You should be sure you mean it when you say that you will be pleased to have the governing body discuss any school policy causing widespread concern.

3   You can, when parent-governor elections are imminent, have a meeting with parents to talk about the role of the governing body, and what it is and isn't appropriate to expect of parent representatives. Do, however, be positive about the *governing body's* right to question any school policy or general practice if there is a problem with it, and the individual governor's right to bring up any matter of *general* concern. You can at the same meeting advertise your half-hour session. Don't expect big attendances for either at first. But the effect will be healthy: sometimes a diminution of concern proves how right you were to respond to it; people relax when they know the door is open. That isn't failure.

4   You can encourage as much openness as possible about any change affecting the school which is already being discussed by the governing body – never of course before such discussion takes place. It will almost certainly get out, there will be rumours and misinformation, and individual governors will be under great pressure if they are not free to discuss it. Remember that classifying any item of governors' work as confidential is intended to protect individual privacy, not to suppress discussion of general matters affecting the running of the school.

Avoid typecasting

Typecasting may give experts too much say   One sure way of setting governing bodies on the wrong path (and it is widely practised) is typecasting their members. You may well feel that you should encourage your accountants onto the finance committee; your human resource manager onto staffing; and nurses, surveyors or builders onto health and safety, if you are lucky enough to recruit such treasures. This is often overdone. I know many heads whose light at the end of the tunnel is to attract people with a professional skill who will in effect be unpaid advisers to the school on some of its new responsibilities. True the school has a legal responsibility to try its best to recruit someone from the business community, but I don't think the idea was to get free professional advisers, rather, surely, to give the whole governing body a necessary perspective from the world of business. An important reason for avoiding typecasting is that it threatens governors' corporate responsibility and the equal valuation of every member, thereby creating A and B teams (dealt with later).

It may also encourage too much detailed checking   Typecasting may well bring about a situation where 'checking-up' on the school becomes excessive and strategic concepts are lost. Perhaps you need to remind your governors that, much as we all welcome a bit of expertise when we don't understand something, the role of experts is to make the task do-able by lay people, not to do it for them, and that in any case governors should not be too much involved in day-by-day surveillance.

Keeping governors ahead of the action

Finally among variations on the role confusion theme comes the governing body which only ever seem to approve (i.e. legitimise) actions which have already taken place, decisions already made, thinking too far advanced to change, statements or policies which are already in final written form. They say they are just rubber stamps and often imply that this is a deliberate attempt to marginalise their role. I doubt whether it is often deliberate. It is just how things have been done for a long time, and governors are not blameless, since they often sit passively waiting to be told what they have to make decisions on.

But regardless of where blame lies, it is heads who have the power to rescue governors from the 'rubber-stamping role', firstly by regularly providing them with information about future events and requirements, secondly by weaving teacher-talk and governor-talk more closely together within the school.

> *The first of these aims is achieved by heads covering in their report to each governing body meeting not only details of staff changes, pupil achievements, visitors, excursions and other past happenings, but at least a paragraph flagging up new government initiatives, changes in the catchment area, coming deadlines, expected circulars, dates of council meetings, and other events calling for governors' responses. Governors can then review their meeting dates, set up working parties, collect information, and so be ready. (See Chapter 8 for more detail on this.)*
>
> *The second objective is achieved by encouraging small groups of governors with an interest in a particular subject to attend staff meetings when a change or an initiative is at the brainstorming stage, and arranging for more teachers to talk about their work at governors' committees. Lay people can often contribute more at the stage when principles are being debated than they can when the proposal reaches the fine-tuning stage. They will also understand the project better as it develops and feel that they share ownership of the outcomes. (Again, more detail in Chapter 8.)*

2. Achieving equal status for all members of a governing body and helping them to work together

This section covers the problems of an over-dominant chair, avoiding A and B teams, and promoting fair distribution of the workload. Chapter 3 has a great deal to say about the absence of any power vested in the individual governor and the vital importance to the governing body of understanding its corporate role. But the importance of the corporate principle extends far beyond the proper respect for territory and the need to restrain over-zealous solo performers. When members do not 'think corporate' it encourages all forms of power drift within the governing body, and power drift embraces a wide range of dysfunctions which to many heads and governors seem difficult to cure.

Avoiding 'power drift'

The governing body's corporate role must always be protected. By 'power drift' I mean all those situations where the corporate power of the governing body has been allowed to slide, perhaps into the lap of one powerful person (sometimes, but not invariably the chair), perhaps to a small powerful group. Governors often talk about A and B teams, referring to the disturbing sense many have of a governing body clearly divided into insiders and outsiders, the former being those who know more, have more influence, get the high-profile tasks and may even meet on their own sometimes. This is discussed below. It isn't only power which sometimes seems to be unequally distributed but work and responsibility, the worst form being where one group has the power and another the work! Often new governors sense these inequalities as soon as they join a governing body and are discouraged by them. This underlines the need for a good *induction procedure* (*see* Chapter 5) – new governors often feel that they will never be considered for the A team. Always remember that although these issues look difficult they often respond to simple nuts-and-bolts remedies. Some of these are described below.

> *Remember too that the exercise of too much power by an individual or small group is rarely restrained by direct means, but much more commonly by empowering other participants. This is an approach particularly suitable in headteachers' relationships with the governing body, since they will not wish to intervene overtly.*

A dominant chair

Remember that in current education law the chair has very little power as an individual. Many are still working to an older model, but today's model is much more of a team-builder role, with no power to make decisions on your own except in an emergency like a fire or a flood. Often the relationship between the chair and the head is too close. True, most heads value a chair who is a special friend, someone you can confide in without commitment when worried, someone to try ideas on. But if this relationship ever threatens the team spirit of the governing body you should take it seriously and do what you can to put the situation right. Apart from the importance to the school of a fully functional governing body, you have to remember that you personally are very much exposed if you don't have their corporate support, and also that decisions which are not made corporately are not legal and could backfire.

If the relationship is very close you are the best person to remind the chair of the need to involve everybody in the formation and ownership of policies, to work openly, to ensure that issues don't appear to have been sewn up before they are ever discussed. You can also quietly encourage other governors to take on particular responsibilities, build relationships with committee chairs and other members, promote work-sharing policies and even gently open up debate at meetings of the governing body. There are many ways discussed elsewhere in the book of developing involvement of all governors in the school and ensuring that faces other than the chair's become familiar to pupils and staff through sharing out ceremonial tasks. Good planning (remembering what was said about flagging up future issues in your reports) can make it less likely that the chair will be driven to make (illegal) decisions between meetings.

In short, the moment that you begin to suspect that the style of the chair is damaging the corporate working of the governing body there are many quiet steps you can take to help build up the contribution of other members again. Always be sensitive to signs of resentment, encourage the chair to promote open discussion, and if the two of you have had prior discussion of any matter make sure that this is reported to the whole governing body and so presented as to leave governors completely free to debate the issue.

A and B teams

New governors especially sometimes get the immediate impression of an A and a B team, a situation in which a group of more influential governors dominate the work. The perceived divide may be based on length of service, social class, race, knowledge of the school or the bigger world or closeness to the head, and even if there is no divide, and the A team exists only in the eyes of the B team beholder, the perception is still divisive. This is a feature of many governing bodies which are not working well, and it can be solved by good induction, working processes designed to give everyone equal status, and above all regular overhaul of roles and groupings. The head personally can do a great deal to make every member of the governing body important.

Starting right

A good induction procedure is essential, since the new governor needs to feel part of the action (and the relationships, in-jokes, in-language, social acceptance) from the beginning: this is fully covered in Chapter 5. The procedure should in particular provide for new governors to be invited to sample all committees as observers for a while so that they can judge where they would like to offer their services and be brought into active participation as soon as possible. Everything that is done and said in the presence of a new governor gives messages about the unity of the group and the equality of all participants, however, and if all concerned remember this, it is halfway to making the governing body seem an open and friendly institution.

Fair and open procedures

The governing body should be careful to demonstrate that choice of committee members and governors to do specific jobs is by open election, not achieved through some kind of power network which the newcomer doesn't understand. All the conventions about how people address each other should give the message of equality and any unfamiliar terms should be translated as a matter of course. You as headteacher can have a great deal of influence and you are quite likely to be the most experienced person around the table at making a variety of people feel welcome.

The main way of shaking out established inequalities is to *overhaul all working-together procedures regularly*. Regulations now require governors to review their committee arrangements annually, and I believe that at the *first meeting of the school yea*r – which is an opportunity often wasted – this should be extended to all the governing body's working practices and the rules it sets for its members. In February or May members can't easily bring up current problems without personal embarrassment because they have name tags on them, but in September or October, if you all see this as a formal tidying-up time, you have ways of dealing as a group with:

- over-dominant chairs;
- cliques;
- inappropriate behaviour by one or more members;
- school visiting arrangements;
- confidentiality rules;
- how individual governors are chosen for tasks;
- work-sharing of all kinds.

You yourself can be watchful for any tendency for a few individuals to hog the discussion or anyone to be excluded, and warn the chair if you don't feel able to handle it yourself. And remember that you are just as free as others whom I advise to use the magic sentence 'Please could we all discuss that?' or 'Please could we go round the table and make sure everybody is happy about that?' whenever agreement seems to be too easily assumed.

Sharing of the work

Another kind of divided body is one where a small number bear the load of attendance, paperwork, decision-making and involvement in the school. This causes great resentment, but sometimes those outside feel unhappy and don't know how to get in. There are also situations where resentment builds up because a few governors are poor attenders, don't prepare properly for meetings and resist doing their share of the work. In Chapter 2 I have written at length about how a governing body should demonstrate high expectations of all its members and set standards they expect from each other. I would like to see heads also become a little more willing to show their disappointment when promises are broken, especially promises to participate in events which encourage the pupils, but I know some find this hard. Otherwise the best remedy is still to adopt clear work-sharing arrangements and return to them often, and this you *can* gently encourage. Indeed, in every way the best use of your close relationship with the chair is to put your considerable influence behind all the procedures and conventions which reflect the equality of all governors and their equal right – and duty – to contribute.

3. Clear shared aims

Last of all, successful relationships between the head and governors and within the governing body require clearly understood common purposes, principles and priorities. That means that you have to communicate scrupulously well to produce the school's policies ('So what is this policy for – cheapness, equality, justice?'). You all have to be explicit about the aims of the school itself when drawing up and revising key planning and publicity documents (development plan, annual report, prospectus).

Taking time to share your beliefs and priorities

But above all you must make *time* in all that you do to share the things that brought you together and the things that keep you at it. Too many governing bodies behave like a motorist with brakes out of control, looking for something cheap to hit. They study just the right-hand column of figures, looking for a figure which roughly corresponds to what they have to save. £30,000? Great, don't fill that drama post. Or let's postpone the enlargement of the library. Have they ever discussed the importance of drama in the curriculum? By what standards was the library considered deficient? Where in their priorities does the library figure? They've never discussed those things. Many bad decisions are made that way, and time *must* be found to return to fundamental principles and relate them tirelessly to the task in hand.

How to be less agenda-driven

Some governing bodies have experimented with a second meeting a term which, instead of being an extra business meeting, is concerned with longer-term issues, problems so far unsolved or on the horizon, the background to and thinking behind, changes in legal requirements, the odd really important new book, relationships with neighbouring schools, and much more generally the background to business which is coming up later in the term. Teachers are encouraged to come, there is no pressure to reach agreement, and it does give people a chance to speak rather more freely and communicate more frankly about their feelings and priorities. It is also a valuable learning opportunity.

But even without special occasions governing bodies can easily be encouraged to return to fundamentals at frequent intervals. It focuses their minds. As a former Prime Minister put it 'If you don't have a star to guide you by, you will be prisoners of your agenda'. Well, we don't all have to have the same stars, but if we have none we know all about being agenda-driven. Looking at the stars gives governors a perspective and also makes their little scraps seem trivial.

The essentials of a properly functioning governing body are its common aims and principles; the recognition at all times that those aims and principles are corporate and must be corporately pursued; the equality of all its members, equal in their right to participate and their duty to do their share of the work. People aren't perfect and there are few governing bodies which have never briefly deserted any of these principles, but prompt recognition that there is a problem is usually halfway to a solution.

Because the themes in this chapter are fundamental to the ethos and spirit of a governing body it doesn't lend itself to the sort of medical encyclopaedia approach heads may have expected, with symptoms, ailments and treatments, so I have tried to do something like that in Worksheet 4.1, where some of the common problems and suggested remedies are listed. As I re-read I realise how clearly one message, which wasn't perhaps uppermost in my mind when I began, comes over. That is the often unseen but very powerful influence for good or ill which a headteacher can exercise over many crucial aspects of the governing body's work, aspects which can profoundly affect its harmony and its corporate working. Perhaps I have also realised for the first time the full significance of that initial decision on whether to be a member of the governing body, which every new head has to make, because this profoundly affects the influence he or she can exercise. That is why I dealt with that issue right at the beginning.

Above everything else, however, to make a difference any head must want a strong and effective governing body. The motivation is everything.

Worksheet 4.1:

■ ■ ■

Some quick answers to common problems

> *This paper is a quick reference guide to solving some of the problems discussed in Chapter 4.*

Governors are interfering at too detailed a level – checking up on teachers, questioning punishments, adding up figures, etc.

After talking to chair, if appropriate, do the following:

1 Give them Worksheet 3.1.
2 Discuss roles with them in the light of Chapter 3.
3 Ask your LEA governor training team for an in-house session on roles.
4 Make sure you really do involve them on policy issues underlying managerial decisions and encourage them to question freely at that level.
5 Point them towards strategic issues affecting the problem which concerns them, e.g. give them a short account of how teachers get monitored and supported, seeking their critical comments; ask if they want to revisit behaviour guidelines; describe internal monitoring of budget, etc. Interest them in your managerial arrangements for checking things and invite comment.

Chair is assuming too dominant a role, taking decisions between meetings, cutting discussion short.

1 Don't ask chair for decisions. Ask him/her instead how you can organise reference of matter to governors.

2 Remind chair of governors' powers and warn him/her of dangers of short-cuts when he/she seems to be moving to unilateral action. Show him/her Appendix IV item 5. Refer to fact that decisions made other than correctly can be dangerous and/or expensive if discovered.

3 Ask him/her to let you know if ever he/she thinks you as head rely too much on him/her at the expense of your relationships with other governors.

4 Avoid having to make decisions between meetings by alerting governors to issues on the horizon in time for them to plan their involvement – *see* Chapter 8.

5 Invite committee chairs to the occasional meeting with you and the chair to talk policy – ask chairs to be sure to report discussion to their members.

6 Ask if individual governors can occasionally prepare an item for discussion.

7 At meetings quietly suggest chair goes round table for views on an issue, or ask individuals you know are interested in the subject what they think about an item.

8 Encourage governors to discuss what qualities and kind of relationship with them they are looking for before they elect a chair.

9 With chair's agreement, circulate to all governors a rough note of any informal discussions held outside governors' meetings.

A few governors dominate meetings and overwhelm quiet ones.

1 Try asking individual governors to prepare items for discussion and ask chair to go round table inviting views.

2 Ensure that when time comes to decide on committee membership, governors take it seriously, especially the need to get a good spread of interests and not typecast.

3 Suggest to a friendly governor, perhaps one of your parents, that a few colleagues need befriending or pushing forward.

4 Ask really shy governors to do some small duty in the school, e.g. serving squash after the sponsored walk, helping with parents' evening. Make a point of showing you value all governors.

5 Overhaul your induction procedures. A poor start often produces a permanent B team. (Chapter 5 refers.)

6 Make sure that you yourself are not unconsciously talking more freely to those whom you know best and who are easy to talk to, and ignoring others – we all do it.

A few governors are either poor attenders or dodging the work.

1 Remind chair or likely other governor that you must be formal about apologies now to give effect to attendance rules, and should only accept if there is a good reason.

2   Try asking them to prepare an item for discussion.

3   Make sure your governors have proper work-sharing arrangements and that they are serious about them, revisiting them often.

4   When you invite people to school events, remind them when you see them, make a note if they say they hope to be there, notice them when they turn up.

5   In bad cases, talk to your chair about writing to the appointing body if it is an appointed governor, asking for people who have more time for you when there are vacancies.

Governors complain of being just 'rubber stamps', asked to agree to things already decided or too advanced to change.

1   Chapter 8 refers. Use your regular reports to governors to flag up things they will have to consider before you meet again if they are to be on top of them. Encourage planning around these issues.

2   Arrange for appropriate governors to join staff in discussing policy issues at brainstorming stage.

3   Get key staff to come to governors' meetings (with the governing body's consent of course) to talk about their work and its big issues.

Parent-governors see everything through their own children.

1   Don't be too hard. We waited a long time to have governors who were closely involved in the school with direct personal interest.

2   Try to broaden their horizons through contact with some of the school's more intractable human problems. Watch them develop.

3   Keep them busy and involved.

Governors complain about paper overload.

1   Look carefully at the papers emanating from the school. Could they be crisper, less repetitive, freer from jargon? Are they all necessary?

2   Share out the task of introducing items, giving a governor one item to research and present from time to time.

3   Say in each paper coming to governors whether it is for information, action or comment, and always put in an executive summary.

4   Try your best to substitute observation and experience for paper as a way of briefing governors.

You have evidence of some breach of confidentiality or indiscreet gossip by a governor.

1   Don't pursue the offender directly. Ask the chair if you can have a few minutes to remind governors that most of what they discuss is not confidential, but when something they discuss concerns an individual's private life they must not disclose it to anyone at all.

2   Find an opportunity, e.g. when you are discussing visits to the school, to say that, like teachers, governors have privileged access and hear many funny, sad, revealing things that innocent children say about their family life, and should, like teachers, be professional and keep their counsel.

A governor or group of governors behaves in an inappropriate way. You might hear, for instance, that a governor has been disloyal outside about a corporate decision he/she didn't agree with. Or another has spoken disparagingly about the school to outsiders, or reported a governors' discussion in a way that presented fellow governors in a bad light. Or a group of governors have met in someone's house to discuss some agenda matter, pointedly not telling, say, the teacher governors or the LEA governors about the meeting.

1   Offences against governing body rules or ethics are for the chair, not the head, to deal with. Tell the chair what you know, and hope that he/she will have a word with those concerned.

2   If it is a serious or persistent offence, try to find some indirect way to get it raised as a general matter. The first meeting of the year is a good time for 'housekeeping' matters. Your LEA training team might also have suggestions.

A teacher-governor often puts you on the spot by bringing up a controversial issue at meetings without warning you.

1   Tell the offender, or ask the chair to tell him/her, that you never react badly to frank discussion on the governing body, however challenging, provided that it is a matter within the governing body's competence, not a private grumble or a problem for which there are other remedies, and that you get advanced warning.

2   Make absolutely sure that you *do* react well to teacher-governors' frank interventions, and that you never do anything to make them afraid of warning you. Teacher-governors need to be sure that you won't try to stop them raising a matter, or take it out on them in some other way.

5
■ ■ ■
Finding and Keeping Effective Governors

Headteachers often think that the quality of the governors they get is outside their control. That is one of the reasons why they don't mind telling colleagues about awful governors – unlike awful staff, it doesn't in their eyes reflect badly on their own leadership. I hope to show that headteachers can have an influence on recruitment. They can also contribute to retention and good performance by establishing sound induction processes and seeing that every governor is valued and properly used. In short this chapter is a guide to the practicalities of recruitment, induction and retention.

You can make a difference

Good governors don't come by accident

Everything a good governing body does needs planning. If they lurch from meeting to meeting without plan or direction they are worse than useless: they are actually a brake on the progress of the school. A headteacher who tolerates this situation may not know how to make things better, but the message that head conveys is lack of respect for the governors' role. This may not be intended, and one can easily blame the unremitting pressures on schools in recent years. Heads who find these pressures overwhelming may well see governors as one complication they could do without. But that is not an option, and an ineffective governing body is a millstone round the school's neck. Why do some accept this, when they would agree in another context that if they think something is important they will find time to do it and to do it well? Is it mostly because they assume that the quality of the governors they get is something they can't influence? This is the assumption I want to challenge.

How can I get good governors?

Some of the answers are easy, but the most important one is pretty hard. Here it is.

> *The best recruiting agency is a governing body already doing a job which is real and visible. If parents and others in the school community have the work of the governing body put often before them, and see that it has an impact on school quality, more of them will want to be involved, so there will be a wider choice. Those who take that kind of interest will tend to be eager and committed. If, on the other hand, the governing body is seen to be an irrelevance, few people will want to be governors, and those few may have the wrong motives or lack staying power. It is indeed a sure recipe for recruiting people who just want the status without the work, or have some private kite to fly. Most people have too much sense to join a dud show.*

Visibility

Even if you have an excellent group of governors working effectively you may not be able to guarantee equally good successors if their work is not visible in the school and its community. Therefore visibility is crucial to maintaining the quality. But what if I don't have anything to advertise, you will say? Isn't that a vicious circle? Well, you certainly can't turn a sham of a governing body into something real overnight, but you don't have to do it all at once. There is an instalment system. That's where the visibility comes in. As soon as governors have done one small thing right you can display it in the school. Easy – you have control of the means. Then you have to make sure they do something else right and advertise that. So make up your mind that as soon as you have an issue on which, with your help, the governing body is going to shine, you start planning the visibility. Be generous in giving credit even if you have been a leading player. It could be just a couple of lines in your parents' newsletter saying that your governors have got the Council to agree to put the new drama studio top of their priorities for school building. Or even that they have persuaded *you* to postpone the change in the reading scheme until parents have had a chance to discuss it. The latter also shows that you listen, which is a bonus. Never mind if it's only a small achievement – there's nothing wrong with starting small if you know where you are going.

Ensure that, whenever you have an event well-attended by your parents or community, governors are there with name and role badges, and given a high profile. Use every opportunity to tell people who they are and what they do. Show how you work together but also that they are free to challenge you sometimes if they aren't sure you are right. This last is important. Possible recruits are interested in the quality of the people they will work with and in knowing that the head welcomes a challenge. But even when that is assured, they will want to know, given that they are likely to be busy people if they are any good, that they won't just be cheer-leaders. And as you improve the relevance and quality of what you do together you have more to advertise.

The different categories of governors and how to get good ones

Appointed governors – LEA and foundation

I don't intend to criticise any category of governors – all have good and less good members. The only trouble is that LEAs have to field a very large number of governors – larger than ever from September 1999 – and often have to draw on people who are already very busy and committed. Similarly, when voluntary aided schools have to have enough representatives of the foundation to give a majority of two or three over all other members combined, it puts a big strain in some cases on the community from which they are appointed. The system produces some excellent governors in both LEA and foundation categories and many a school could say that one of these is so involved and able that he or she is the natural leader on the governing body.

However good they are, it's vital they have time In too many other schools, however, simply because in the fields of local government and church administration there are many demands on the able and committed, it can produce people who with the best will in the world just don't have the time that schools need today and become out of touch. Complaints about LEA governors – unfilled vacancies, poor attendance and lack of direct involvement in the school – are too common. There is great variety of experience across the country, because appointing policies differ widely.

If this is not your problem, fine. If it is, remember that anybody has a right to say when something isn't working. There is no reason why your governing body should not approach those who make the appointments and ask for people who are perhaps less influential but also less busy; people who are less experienced but perhaps more lively and energetic; people who are less well-known but more in touch. Go further: make some suggestions of local people who fit the appointing body's criteria and whom you or your governing body see as good school governor material. Remember that if, as a head, you have chosen to be a governor you can play a full part in recruitment strategies. If you have not, and are also not exceptionally devious, you have to stand aside and let your good ideas go to waste. You and your governors may even be able to help broaden your LEA's approach to governor appointments. Increasingly LEAs are abandoning the old party political routes to service on governing bodies and some are even advertising for people with proven interest and commitment. Pressure can speed up that process.

Church appointing bodies are also increasingly looking for representatives from young families in the church community rather than seasoned stalwarts as governors, and now that they are required to include more parents among their representatives there will be many changes. Here too suggestions are often welcome.

In Appendix III you will find a brief guide to the composition of governing bodies since September 1999, following the implementation of the School Standards and Framework Act of 1998.

Co-opted governors

Here, providing you think often about recruitment and not just when there is a vacancy, you have much more scope. In community (formerly county) schools co-optees are the largest single group. Governors should *always* be seeking interested and promising local people to recruit when the time comes, and there are governing bodies which at any time will have the odd one or two invited as observers to see what it is like. Talk often with your governors about the sort of people you need to maintain a good balance. If most governors are very local and nearly all present or past parents, well, you could be very lucky, so appreciate it. But if you feel a bit cosy and inbred, look for someone from a completely different background who will challenge you and shake you up a bit. If, on the other hand, you haven't got much localness and direct commitment, find it, keep it and cherish it, because there's nothing else so important.

Ensure that you don't, in your eagerness to sign people up, give them a false idea of the time commitment involved. In the long run if you con them into agreeing by saying it's only three meetings a year and the harvest festival, you may risk getting people who are not very good or just in it for their CVs. Others may be very good but unlikely to stay long when they know how much time it takes. Make sure that your own governors tell them the sort of involvement which you all consider essential – not forgetting to add how addictively interesting it is. Governors may find interviewing a co-optee helpful, not so much as an aid to selection as to secure realism and understanding on their part. You can also take the initiative – and remember what I said above about much of this depending on whether you are a governor yourself – in encouraging local employers to follow the good practice of the best, i.e. taking the provision of governors seriously and being proud to contribute, giving generous time off and even in a few cases supporting training.

Parent-governors

Here you need a good field and a lot of participation to get quality. Sometimes likely candidates are put off by not knowing much about it and then being sent a formal, even legalistic, letter which sounds like a rate demand. How much better if, in addition to writing a friendly letter yourself, you let the retiring parent-governor or another keen one send them a photocopied note in their own words and their own hand, especially in an area where levels of formal education are low, and keen and good people may lack the confidence to stand. Look at Worksheet 5.2: this is a real letter used by one school to recruit a new parent-governor, but the names are fictitious.

Remember especially here what I said first about recruitment depending on making the job real. If you haven't a very good record in making parent-governors welcome, supporting them in their representative role and appreciating what they do in that role, even if it's sometimes inconvenient, the news will soon get round and parents will be reluctant to become involved in something so difficult. Conversely, if your parents know that you are generous in the encouragement you give parent-governors to bring general parent concerns to the governing body and communicate with other parents, you have a big advantage in recruiting.

Teacher-governors

Much the same considerations apply to teacher-governors. The quality and the active contribution of teacher-governors differ enormously and from my observation the attitude of the headteacher to teacher representatives is the main variable. Heads tend to get the teacher-governors their own attitudes encourage and some suffer as a result. You will get the best representation:

- if the election is seen as important and attracts lively interest;
- if teacher-governors know that their representatives will be encouraged to bring staff concerns on matters of policy to the governing body, and report back non-confidential matters in the staffroom;
- if teacher-governors are not afraid to express their views freely in governors' meetings even if they are different from yours, being completely confident that their careers will not be affected.

If these conditions are not met you will tend to get low participation and not attract the best quality candidates. This would be a pity, since good teacher-governors can be a tremendous strength to the school. They not only raise staff morale by demonstrating that staff concerns get a hearing and that decisions about their working lives are made openly and fairly, which is itself a strength to the school, but they also provide enrichment of governors' understanding of curriculum matters, even if it is at some cost in terms of conformity and predictability. Surely you can live with that?

The best you as a head can do, therefore, to ensure high quality teacher-governors, is convince the staff that it is a job worth doing, supported by you, and deserving of their best talent.

Induction

The general standard of induction of newcomers is appalling, not just on governing bodies but in many other working and social groups in the community. Too many governors report that they arrive at their first meeting with no form of briefing and find it cold and bewildering. If they are parents they will as a minimum know the head, be familiar with the building, and probably know a few of their colleagues. At the other extreme a new LEA or co-opted governor may know nobody, will wander round looking for rooms with a light on, won't know where not to sit, and won't say a word. Between these extremes many will sit there trying to pick up the names, the relation-ships, the 'in-words' and jokes, the acronyms and the background to long-running issues, as they go along. Some governors use each others' first names. The newcomers aren't sure whether all do. Between meetings they will receive papers but may not speak to a soul. It isn't that we are rude and unsociable and that newcomers are not welcome. *It is just that it is nobody's job and there is no plan for getting it done.* Everybody should play a part, ideally inspired and co-ordinated by the chair. It certainly doesn't all rest on the head's shoulders, though the head is well placed to point out the need for a plan if necessary and suggest governors discuss it.

Making every step somebody's job is all that is needed, given that no offence is ever meant and that nobody wants to waste all that potentiality. Like every-thing else the governing body does, it needs planning. Ideally the head, the chair and at least one ordinary governor (link governor or mentor perhaps, if these are part of your system) should separately contact the new recruit before the meeting. The head should ask new governors to call as soon as the name is known, welcoming them to the school, giving them basic documents like the prospectus, a plan of the building and a list of staff with their responsibilities, and offering a warm welcome to visit again soon and look at some aspect of the school at work.

The chair should at least telephone and make them welcome and perhaps sketch some of the governors' current main preoccupations. The link governor (some LEAs have these to communicate both ways about training opportunities/needs) or mentor (you can introduce this idea yourselves if you wish) should meet them face to face for tea or coffee, offer to go to the first meeting (or a training session) with them, lend them a helpful book, and generally try to demystify the role. At the meeting a short social session breaks the ice to begin with, then the chair should publicly introduce the new governor, and other members should (loudly) say a bit about themselves. Acronyms and jargon should be elucidated if they can't be avoided, the background to long-running issues should be filled in, and the newcomer welcomed to sit in on as many committees and working groups as possible for a while to see what would interest them. That procedure should be a minimum, yet new governors at training sessions regularly say that it doesn't happen.

A mentor is quite a good idea as long as the job is spread around and it is for a limited time. It is always a help to someone who has a lot of questions to know that *it's somebody's job* to respond. I keep returning to 'somebody's job' but it really is fundamental. In a school where relations between governors and staff are as good as they should be, you may like to pair a new governor with a staff member, so that there's someone to solve mysteries about school routines and processes. Worksheet 5.3 sets out all this.

Retention

The way the governing body is treated

The whole of this book could be said to be an answer to the question: 'How do we keep good governors once we have found them?' There's no trick to it that can be conveyed in a few sentences, and every good practice that we adopt makes us a little harder to say goodbye to.

The job must be **real** A governing body which knows that its job is real and valued by the school is likely to keep its members. Normal people don't get pleasure from charades or from territorial warfare, and will soon find some way of spending their evenings where the chairs are more comfortable and the atmosphere pleasanter. Indeed you could almost predict that, if the governing body is a pretence, you will get people without substance, role players, people who like feeling important without doing much; if it's a territorial battlefield you will get people who thrive on conflict and have battles of their own to fight; if it's a shambles you will get ditherers; and if it is not treated with respect you are unlikely in the end to keep people worthy of respect. Positively, a governing body with a real job to do, taken seriously, treated with respect, well organised, and with a common purpose, is more likely to attract *and keep* members who are committed, sincere, hard-working, efficient and purposeful.

The way the governing body works

Next in importance to how the insiders treat the individual comes the teamwork and the sense of equal value among the governors themselves. It is essential that the old hands keep asking themselves whether everybody is contributing, sharing information, sharing responsibility, listening, and being loyal. Nothing drives people away more surely than a suspicion of A and B teams. The chair's leadership is, of course, central in all this, but the head also plays a major part in spotting and trying to correct the kinds of dysfunction covered in Chapter 4, where all these problems are covered. In one sense the head is even more important, since not even the warmest and most democratic of chairs can counter the pervading chill emanating from a head who doesn't accept and value the governors as allies and equals. There's also the difference that the governing body can choose another chair next autumn.

So the first requirement, if you are to retain good governors, is that every governor should have a part to play and a distinctive contribution to make. This cements the commitment and makes it more likely that overwork or passing frustration will not lead them to giving it all up. Even though the power and responsibility are one and indivisible, these are maintained in health when they rest on the varied contributions of equal partners. The tension between corporate responsibility and individual equality is the most distinctive feature of the governing body, and it is just one more talent of our first-class head to recognise and preserve the strong traditions and processes which underpin it.

'And processes' you notice. We will never move far from the nuts and bolts. These nuts and bolts will play a major part in the chapters that follow. Appendix II is a description of the new composition of governing bodies, Worksheet 5.1 suggested an 'audit' system to encourage you to keep a record of your governors' experience, skills and qualities and keep it updated; Worksheet 5.2 is the specimen letter from the retiring parent-governor; and Worksheet 5.3 is an *aide-mémoire* on induction processes.

Looking forward

I began by saying that a head could influence the quality of governors recruited. That is perhaps for some readers a surprising claim, but I believe it is well-founded and that its acceptance could create stronger governing bodies. I have stressed how important it is to provide effective and thoughtful induction for new governors. Finally I have painted a picture of the sort of governing body on which members will be proud to serve and therefore offer commitment and loyal service.

The concerns of the remaining chapters – teamwork, helping governors to become familiar with the school, communication, planning and school improvement – need firm foundation. I hope that I have convinced you that policies for recruitment, induction and retention of governors are essential starting points for the development of the effective governing body, and that introducing them in the individual school is one more important job for the wise headteacher.

Worksheet 5.1

. . .

My governors: A personal *aide-mémoire*

This is an aid to maintaining and refreshing your knowledge of your governors as individuals. It will help you to appreciate and use the experience and talents they have to offer, and value them as people. Omit anything which might be considered private, or anything you would not show them. The aim is a good and productive relationship. Fill in the minimum at first, and add as you get to know them. Three imaginary examples follow.

Proforma

Name	Type of governor	Date joined us
Address	Telephone	Occupation

Parent or past parent?

Experience, skills, contacts, etc.

Personal qualities

Example 1

Name	Type of governor	Date joined us
Eileen Mackay	Parent	October 1998

Address	Telephone	Occupation
4, Beechtree Crescent	H 0123 123 4567	Doctor's receptionist
Townend	W 0123 8901234	(part-time)
Carlton AB4 2BC		

Parent or past parent?
Gordon in Year 4, Amy in Reception. An older son, Sam, left in 1998. Mrs Mackay attended the school herself .

Experience, skills, contacts, etc.
Before she had her children Mrs Mackay worked full-time at Carlton Hospital as a nurse. She also has secretarial skills which she has kept up to date. Her husband is a well-respected small builder working mostly in the locality. She is very much involved with MENCAP, having had a mentally handicapped daughter, Rose, between Sam and Gordon: Rose died at 12. Qualified first-aider.

Personal qualities
A very much respected member of the local community. Caring, hard-working and thoroughly practical. A good listener, indeed has all-round skills with people. Never refuses to help with any good cause. Also thinks clearly and is single-minded in putting the interests of children first. Helps in the school with crafts and cooking. Runs a first-aid club with juniors.

Example 2

Name	Kind of governor	Joined us
Alan Cambridge	Co-opted	June 1997 (casual vacancy when Mo Selby resigned because of workload)

Address	Telephone	Occupation
The Cedars, Church Walk, Carlton, AB1 X 23	H 0123 321 5678 W 3456 654 8765	Personnel officer Menumasters Catering

Parent or past parent ?
One daughter, Abigail, now grown up, attended the school.

Experience, skills, contacts, etc.
Has ten years' experience in present post, having taken the IPD Diploma by part-time study in 1988 and worked for a year or two in another catering firm. Thoroughly versed in employment law and personnel practice, and also now knows a great deal about contract catering. His company is very large. Excellent IT skills.

Personal qualities
An intelligent and conscientious governor, and after past experience of trying to recruit expert help we are delighted he seems to have time for us and is a 100% attender. Keen to learn more about education, as well as ready to advise on personnel issues. Good clear thinker. Willing to help start computer club if there is sufficient interest. Company staff have half-day on Wednesdays as they work Saturday am, and Alan seems willing to get involved with school activities.

Example 3

Name	Kind of governor	Joined us
John Parrish	LEA	September 1996

Address	Telephone	Occupation
15, Briar Cottages Meadowsend, Nr. Carlton. UV 4 5 AB	H 0123 654 3210	Retired village postmaster

Parent or past parent

Two grandchildren in years 5 and 6. Own three children attended the school thirty years ago.

Skills, experience and contacts

Knows almost every family within five miles of Carlton, including the farming community. Has been a councillor for eight years. Limited formal education, but intelligent and full of common sense. A beautiful pianist, self taught. Natural skill with figures, and recently appointed chair of Finance, following a disappointing experience with a qualified accountant. Never fails to turn up to a school event, but shy of coming into classes.

Personal qualities

A rather modest man, undervaluing his qualities. Thoroughly honest and sensible, with a wealth of understanding of local people and fond of children. Very quiet at meetings and says he finds some of the documents very difficult. Said to sing very well, especially Gilbert and Sullivan.

Worksheet 5.2
■ ■ ■

Finding a successor

The attached letter was written by a real parent-governor at the end of her term of office, with the encouragement of the head. It was in her own hand, and was photocopied and sent to every parent by child post. Fictitious names and places have been substituted. It is suggested as an alternative to the usual formal notification of a vacancy, in the belief that a hand-written letter in homely style is more likely to encourage parents who are nervous or unsure about what they may be taking on.

35, New Road,
Greysone,
Near Melford

From Margie Sadler

20 March 1998
Dear parents,

You elected me as your parent-governor in 1994 and I hope you know that I have done my best to look after parents' interests. The school has seen many changes and Mrs Winfield has involved us in everything.

Now, sadly, my four-year term is up, and because my youngest Josie leaves to start the comprehensive later this year I shall not stand again. The reason I am writing is that we need a new parent-governor and there will be elections next term. I want to tell you a bit about the job and encourage you to stand, as it is very important for the school and all your children.

I will not say it is not a lot of work but it has truly been the most interesting time of my life. Apart from the meetings twice a term we have committees and I was on two, finance and school activities. Besides that we observe lessons and sometimes join in teachers' working parties. Everybody is very friendly and nothing is too hard to understand or else they explain it. Remember I was able to put our concern about the new reading scheme to the staff and also your opinions on the changes in the playground lay-out, and from that a meeting was put on for all parents to discuss the reading, and the plan for the playground was altered a bit.

Apart from that we had an OFSTED inspection with a good report and we have made a plan to improve the few things they drew to our attention. We wrote new guidelines on discipline this term and also decided to close the two doors at the back of the school except for times when the children will be arriving or leaving when they will be supervised.

Sorry this may be a bit more of a walk for any from the Melford Road side who come late but it is for our children's safety. We also moved the reception office so the front door is always in view.

Geoff Abraham and Patsy Conner the other parent-governors will still be on the board. Do please consider standing. It is truly very interesting and no need to be afraid. You never have to make any decision by yourself because we work as a team and there is always expert advice to hand if we ask for it.

Yours truly,

Margie Sadler

Figure 5.1: Letter from an out-going governor to parents

Worksheet 5.3

■ ■ ■

A good induction process

1 The head is told the name of the new governor(s). He/she invites them to come into school and welcomes them. He/she gives them a few really basic documents – a plan of the school building, a list of all staff with their responsibilities (e.g. head of modern languages, Year 5 class teacher, teacher responsible for literacy, welfare assistant, bursar, midday supervisor) and perhaps the prospectus. He/she invites each newcomer to fix a day to come in and watch some aspect of the school at work. She shows them the room where governors usually meet.

2 The chair telephones or calls on the new governors, thanks them for agreeing to serve, makes them welcome, tells them about some of the current and long-running issues.

3 An ordinary governor (possibly the link governor or a nominated mentor) invites the new governor(s) to a cup of tea or coffee, talks to them in a friendly way about the governing body, offers to call for them to go to the first meeting or a training session, lends them a book he/she has found helpful. He/she tells them a bit about how the governing body arranges its work.

4 At the meeting – which could incorporate a short social session with a drink and a sandwich – the chair formally welcomes the new governor(s) and says a bit about them. Then each governor introduces him or herself fully and audibly. Throughout the meeting the chair explains any jargon or acronyms and sketches the background to any long-running issues. He/she tells the newcomer what committees and working groups the governing body currently has, and how many a governor would normally be involved in. He/she suggests that the new governor(s) should go straight away to as many as possible just to listen. If governors normally use first names with each other, the newcomer(s) should be included from the start.

5 A mentor governor for a time is a good idea: people don't mind bothering a colleague with questions if they feel it's part of the system. If relations with teachers are close and good you could also link a new governor with a teacher for a time to deal with questions about school organisation.

6 These are just suggestions. There are other good systems. The important thing is that there is a plan, and that new governors feel at home right from the beginning.

6

■ ■ ■

Involving Governors in the School

Let us assume that the school is recruiting the best governors available, with some help from the approaches suggested in Chapter 5. You personally are highly motivated to make them a great strength to the school and you communicate high expectations to them in every way you know. You are clear about the role of the governing body and your own, and in particular you recognise how essential it is for them to understand the appropriate level for their input and the corporate nature of their responsibility. To this end you may arrange for a team training session or identify some appropriate training material for them. You will have made sure that all concerned have had a friendly welcome and some basic information about the school. So far so good.

This chapter is about involving governors in the life of the school. It contains some practical suggestions to choose from, and your choice will depend on your school's needs and circumstances and to some extent the character of your governors. You may think my aims are more ambitious than you can yet support, and as I often say to governors we must all move forward from where we find ourselves, not let the brightness of somebody else's distant horizons dazzle us. Before I go on to practicalities, I want to do two things. One is to make clear what I see as the purpose of it all. I don't want you to think I see being a governor as some sort of life-absorbing hobby for people with the time who enjoy that sort of thing. I know well that even if they have the time, you haven't much. I also know that the average governor will greatly enjoy a limited amount of personal contact, and beyond that may want to know why it's important. My second aim is to highlight briefly the changing patterns of employment and leisure which affect people who might like to be governors, and suggest that if we want them to be involved in the school's daily life we may have to accept a less wide range of people to recruit from.

Why is it important?

Not just a hobby

I know most heads welcome governors' interest in the life of the school and sometimes regret that there are some they don't see between meetings. I know most governors, given a chance, enjoy being with the children and find schools fascinating places. But those are not the reasons I spend so much time insisting that every governing body should have their own (realistic) policy about members' participation and put some pressure on themselves to maintain at least a minimum level of school contact.

Knowledge of the school is vital

By law governors make important strategic decisions affecting children and their teachers. Those decisions ought to be caring, considered, soundly based in knowledge, free from prejudice. I find it hard to believe that any governor, however intelligent, however experienced in the world outside, however used to making high-level decisions, can exercise the sort of judgement needed without some understanding of how your school works, how the children learn and behave, what it's like being a teacher. I'm sure many governors agree.

A conflict of aims?

One of the other things we all want, of course, is a governing body representative of our local community. How compatible is this with recruiting governors whose circumstances enable them to become involved in the life of the school? A fully representative governing body may, for various reasons, be an ideal we have to compromise with to some extent anyway. There are areas, for instance, where social problems create large numbers of people without the confidence, basic skills – or even the bus fare – and we must do all we can to improve opportunities for these people both in our schools and our communities. But there are also complex and changing patterns of work and leisure across the social classes which affect choice and make the ideal representation difficult to achieve.

Things that make it easier to recruit

Some of these changes benefit school governor recruitment – far more people whose working lives end early, far more self-employed or employed and working from home, growth in flexitime, statutory increases in holiday entitlement, and above all a growing number of companies giving generous support to employees who are school governors. These factors are already, from my very unscientific observation, bringing us some promising recruits, ordinary people who are both representative of local communities and in a position to spend a little time getting to know the school.

Things that make it harder

Against that there are many, though by no means all, areas of England and Wales where there is virtually full employment. Here the roads get worse and eat up time, life in cities gets more stressful, more women are at work, more people probably travel further to work as a result of mergers, takeovers and the decline of manufacturing in favour of service industries. Above all, parts of the working world get more fiercely competitive, and it is often said that one sector of the population with insufficient work is balanced by another working absurdly long hours to survive in a climate where insecurity and the fear of redundancy are ever-present. This last category must contain many very able and highly motivated people who could very well want to be school governors – but on a limited contract as it were.

Professional skills no substitute

My problem is that I couldn't honestly recommend anyone to take on governorship if they say they could *never* spend time in the school to gain the necessary understanding of it, even if they are able and creative, bring professional skills like accountancy to the task, can acquire gifts and favours for the school from business, or have immense managerial acumen. However welcome, there is a danger that these attributes, if valued above commitment, local knowledge and time, will become an end rather than a means, They may even lead to more 'ordinary' but essentially well-equipped governors being undervalued.

No trade-off

I have spoken to a number of people in my work with governors who don't mind admitting that evening meetings have to be the limit of their contact. I have sometimes offended them. They want me to accept that they contribute something very special in the 'donation' of high level and extremely marketable expertise at meetings, and do so gladly, but they can't get into the school during the day. With all my fears about making decisions in a vacuum, making finance or human resources or law an end in themselves, missing the point of it all and possibly creating a new kind of A team into the bargain, I have said that for me there isn't a trade-off of this kind. That's what I really believe. If you find this an extreme point of view it's as well I am saying it at the outset. It arises partly from my deep conviction that the most ordinary people with commitment and involvement can improve schools, of course. It also reflects the profound respect I have for those who manage schools and teach children, which makes it hard for me to value anything as much in a governor as the desire to understand the life of the classroom and allow it to illuminate every decision. If the worthy aim of recruiting governors from all sections of the working population means that some have to be excused *any* involvement in the school at work, I personally would think the price too high. To me there are insights that no amount of native wit or experience in the outside world can replace.

I don't seek to impose this personal view: how could I anyway when the law makes no such demands and every governing body has to evolve its own standards to meet local circumstances? All I ask is that governors take the point seriously, think about what is most important to them and make their expectations clear to likely recruits.

Forward with the governors we've got

Real induction begins

From now on you will be helping the governing body to develop as an effective team, which is the subject of Chapter 7, and to establish sound working processes (Chapter 8). You will also want to achieve good communication between staff and governors (Chapter 9). But the first step in this long-term induction programme is to make governors familiar with the school. It is a Forth Bridge task, for governors come and go and some forget, and the school itself changes. But it is a vital task if you want their decisions to be based on a real understanding of the aims of your school, your hopes and fears for it, how it is organised, its learning programme, staff and pupils. Appropriate reading can carry governors quite a long way, but, ideally, reading is only a supplement to observation. Even when time is at a premium I am concerned to make best use of very little. Understanding of the school depends not on the time involved but how governors focus and use the time they can spare.

Bird's eye view

Governors who have or have recently had children at the school will already know a great deal about it. Indeed it isn't always the professionals imported by nomination or co-option, and respected for their expertise or experience in the outside world, who risk being seen as the A team. Sometimes these are the ones to feel inadequate beside the easy familiarity of the local people (who are often regularly in and out of the school) with the school and each other.

Everybody should have their guide to the law, the development plan, the school prospectus and the last annual report to parents, any OFSTED reports and action plans, governors' agreed school policies, a plan of the building and a list of all staff with their responsibilities. The last is immensely important:

without knowing roughly what everybody does, you can go seriously wrong. I have never forgotten a parent whose child had become a school refuser because of some unhappy incident in the playground. The mother was deeply upset, so of course I asked her first whom she had talked to about it. 'What's the good?' she said, 'You can't go higher than the dinner lady.' I thought it was so sad that she had abandoned all her opportunities of redress because she didn't know the pecking order in schools.

A basic document There is already a document in many schools which could be an excellent introduction for new governors – the description sent to applicants for teaching posts. I include two as Worksheet 6.2, one primary, one secondary. There's nothing special about them in themselves, though for just a five minute read they are good value. The special thing is that these schools had the bright idea of giving them to new governors as well. That's really getting the most out of the time and skill involved in writing them.

Reading the child post

When my youngest child left the school and I became a co-opted governor I really missed the weekly newsletters and other communications that I used to rescue from the washing machine, simply because I realised how much they kept me in touch with the life of the school. I mentioned this to the head and in no time at all we started getting a little batch of newsletters, reminders about course work, details of school trips, not specially posted but slipped in with any other governor documents which were going out. Another way of achieving the same object is to have a cardboard folder for each governor in the school office with the governor's name on, and into this is slipped routinely a copy of everything that goes out by child. It only takes a minute and – this is the bonus point – governors living nearby may like to come in and empty it now and then, rather than wait for the next mailing.

Getting closer

A simple idea, particularly suitable for a primary school, is for the governors to meet in a different classroom each time. Yes, it does mean moving furniture, but the spin-off can be considerable. Nothing short of actually coming into lessons brings you closer to the children in that year and what they are learning. There will be work on the walls and left around. If the teacher knows it's his/her turn, the room will be extra tidy and attractive and the work up-to-date and well-displayed. There will be all sorts of other pictures and artefacts related to the curriculum. And couldn't you invite the class teacher if he/she wishes to come in for the first ten minutes and say a bit about the class and what they are doing? At the very least it reminds governors that they are going to talk about a living school and not some abstraction.

Visiting the school

I have already referred to the many governors with professional skills who resent the view that contributing expertly to meetings isn't a trade-off against spending time with children at work. In general I am prepared to accept equivalence rather than equality of contribution, but not at the expense of spending some time in the school while it is working if humanly possible. I know that governors, if they are doing their job, already commit an enormous amount of time to it – meetings, doing their share of staff appointments and exclusion hearings, supporting school events, training. In comparison with this the extra time I would envisage asking a governor to spend in the school is very modest, no more than the equivalent of a day a term plus watching out for anything particularly appropriate that a non-teacher could help with. If it is properly planned even half an hour in the school can be an amazing learning experience.

Who can spare the time?

Some heads say 'But my governors all work' as though this was a rare situation. I know that there are a few categories of people whom only legislation can help, legislation to give all governors time off with pay, as a right, to attend to their governor duties. We must go on campaigning for this if we are to get a genuine social spread on governing bodies. At present, the hourly-paid employees of not very community-minded firms, and the small self-employed may find it hard. The former may have pay docked if they stay in for the man coming to repair the washing machine, and may even have little choice when to take their annual holiday. For some among the self-employed a half-day without income is serious. But in many big companies (some supermarkets, some public utilities, some banks especially) employees who are governors get extra leave for their governor duties. We can all do something to advertise and spread this good practice.

Not how much time, but how it's spent It's how the time is spent, not how much, that matters. A governor can spend a day in a big school going into each classroom, shaking the teacher's hand, having coffee and tea with the head and learn almost nothing. He/she can spend half an hour in the staffroom or general office between 8.30 and 9am and get a real feel of the school's life. In the classroom a focus is vital, and going into an interactive type of class makes it possible to join in without, in the end, being noticed. Governors should, of course, always be reminded by the chair that these visits are to learn, not judge, that the teacher must also be clear about this and happy to be visited, and that nothing should be said or done by the visitor during or after the visit which can be construed as intervention or reporting.

Organising the involvement

There should be a framework agreed by the whole governing body for any regular involvement. People mean well, but good habits slip, and I don't think even the most dedicated will get into the school regularly without some kind of attachment system.

It can be a very simple system, like two or three visiting governors every term by appointment. But there are other ways which achieve the same end and something else besides, namely a focus for the visit. The most common is *attaching a governor to a subject area or activity*, following it through with visiting as well as trying to 'specialise' a bit. This is the one I like least but I think it is probably the most common, stimulated I suppose by the advent of special educational needs (SEN)and literacy governors. The specialisation can extend to being the governor who helps with a staff appointment in that subject, talks to the appropriate OFSTED inspector, and so on.

Another method which works excellently in a primary school is *linking a governor (or two) with a class*. It is best if the governor 'goes up' with the class, thus getting to know a group of children well and following their development, seeing the whole curriculum unfold and becoming acquainted with all the staff. This can be a valuable link since the governor can follow a child's progress, mark birthdays and other family events and take part in the class's special events and outings. Again it can be used to decide which governor or governors sit in on staff interviews. I must emphasise that neither this nor any system suggested involves head or staff in any organising. Governors know their commitment, and provided they let the school know when they are planning to visit, make sure it is convenient, and sign in and out, there need be no burden on anyone.

Duty governors

My own favourite attachment system is a period of general duty such as having a duty governor of the month. The rota is fixed a year ahead so that governors can argue, swap and plan. During that month the governor tries to respond to anything the school needs – welcoming an important guest, planting a tree, receiving a cheque from the PTA or a sponsor, covering for the governors any regular meetings of parents or school council to give and receive news, and so on. If the governor can't manage a particular date, he or she must find another governor to take on that task and pay the other governors back in their months. It is thus very realistic, gives everyone a sense of responsibility, spreads the chair's formal duties around and gets more faces known in the school. It also relieves the school of a lot of phoning around when the person earmarked for a task can't come, and is an easy way of finding a governor for a staff appointment if the governing body chooses: the duty governor will find a substitute if he or she is not free.

Finally, the duty governor will go into school for a day or half-day to watch children at work. Some schools use teacher governors to help plan the visits. They know how to match up people who'll get on with each other, can suggest particularly interesting lessons, and help choose a focus and plan for the visit. Worksheet 6.1 is a model communication about the Governor of the Month schedule.

What if teachers are unwilling to be observed?

Governors often ask what to do about teachers who are uncomfortable with governors sitting in on their lessons. 'Have I an automatic right to visit and observe?' they ask. No, they must be told, you haven't. You can visit if the head invites you, *or* if the governors have made a decision which involves individuals in visiting. Having got so far, governors will ask whether either of these alternatives carries the right to go into a classroom where the teacher objects. The answer is that in theory it does, since the head in these (indeed any) circumstances can insist. I then have to give what I consider the real answer, which is that inflicting a governor on a teacher who is hostile or terrified achieves nothing, so is best avoided. Far better to start with the enthusiasts, go on to the willing, proceed to the tolerating, and stop there. It would be different if the object were to inspect, but since it can only be to learn, upsetting a non co-operative teacher is pointless. One can only start with those who have enthusiasm and confidence, and hope that the rest, just as the dry ingredients in a bread dough are drawn by degrees into the fermenting centre, will soon be enthused.

Always to learn, not to judge The head does of course play a part in overcoming the objections of teachers and in all ways promoting the understanding and acceptance of governors' motives. An element in this is reassuring teachers that governors come in to learn, not to inspect, and that it is vital to the important decisions the governing body make that they should know the school well.

Good ideas don't run themselves

It must be emphasised that no system of attachment will last if it is just agreed upon and left to run itself. But the governors must run it themselves. If they don't, participation will be reduced to excessively eager but unstructured visits by a handful of the keenest governors rather than a very modest degree of school involvement for all. Everything worthwhile needs a little planning and managing, and this one will also need a light but timely word now and then about why it was introduced and what the ground rules are. You and the chair must make it clear that whatever system is agreed *must* be realistic for the school and all individual governors, but that once agreed it is a commitment to be honoured to the best of the individual's ability. We are talking here about a governing body culture of expectation which supports its aims and processes.

Other ways of learning

The *written word* and the *visiting* are the main ways in which governors become familiar with the school. They also continue the learning process every time they:

- attend the school's big events;
- read heads' reports;
- study the papers before discussing an issue;
- listen to teachers discussing some aspect of the school's work;
- read, or contribute to, the prospectus, the annual report to parents, the development plan and other key strategic documents.

Any arrangement which brings governors into more direct contact with teachers is good learning experience. It also, of course, promotes better mutual understanding and facilitates the more active involvement of governors in the early stages of policy discussion advocated in Chapter 8.

Schools will have other ideas of their own for familiarising governors with the school.

Active participation – an example

Any activity arranged for the pupils can be fertile ground – an outing, a sponsored walk, a visiting theatre group. My best such experience arose from the sudden staff brainwave of using governors to share the management of feedback by students returning from work experience. 'Management' is too grand a word for what it actually involved, but in fact governors did the job which needed doing, which was essentially that of group facilitator. Each one took a group of ten or so students, helped them fill in a report form, and went on to question them about their experiences, how good their placement had been, what they learned, what they hated, what they'd advise next year's lot ('Have a good breakfast', 'Cover your legs when shampooing a dog', 'Don't imagine hairdressing is glamorous' and 'Wear sensible shoes', 'Don't choose a company by whether you are interested in the product: all the work is low-level so look for something where you might have contact with the public or pick up a skill' were some examples). Then group facilitators and staff met to compare notes, and incidentally there seemed to be agreement that the students who had reported to a governor were especially forthcoming. What governor would fail to find that enjoyable and illuminating? What sensible adult could fail to do it adequately? And for me it beat everything other than sitting in on a teacher appointment as a learning experience.

Worksheet 6.1 illustrates how a school might set out its Governor of the Month arrangements. Worksheet 6.2 gives as examples the documents two closely associated schools (fictitious names) used for teachers applying for posts there, which double up as a general introduction for governors.

> *This chapter has made the point that any governor, to be fully effective, needs to see the school at work. It isn't the amount of time involved – that can be very small – but how it's used and the regularity and consistency which brings the work of governors to life. Heads should expect it. Teachers should welcome it as evidence of governors' interest, obviously, but, much more important, as a contribution to better informed discussion within the governing body of issues on which that body have an influence. As for the governors themselves, involvement with the school at work should form part of the expectations of each other which are at the heart of their work. As such it should be planned and taken seriously by the governing body.*

Worksheet 6.1:

■ ■ ■

Governor of the month schedule

Month	Governor of the month	Special events*
September	Mrs Mackay	Sponsored walk Harvest hamper distribution Year 7 camping weekend
October	Mr Cambridge	Year 8 athletics Theatre workshop visit Year 8 Halloween party
November	Mr Bhag	Dance display Mufti day New parents Q and A evening
December	Miss Halifax	Lunch for senior citizens Visit of Mayor Carols
January	Col. Mann	Year 9 gymnastics display Maths evening PTA dance
February	Mr Parrish	School play Exchange students from Rouen Parents CIT evening
March	Ms Ojaba	School orchestra performance Exchange students from Dresden Year 9 field trip
May	Mr Hoskins	Parents' science evening Mufti day Technology exhibition
June	Mrs Barratt	Records of achievement Options evening
July	Mrs Cranford	School sports Year 11 party

*Events already planned, dates to be announced. Clearly some events we should hope all governors would attend, but even with these we should greatly value the duty governor coming early, welcoming guests, preparing to present certificates, etc. As much notice as possible will be given of additional events. PTA evenings are always the first Monday in the month, students council third Wednesday. Staff briefings 8am Mondays. Would governors of the month kindly arrange classroom observation through teacher-governors?

Worksheet 6.2:

■ ■ ■

Information about the school – two models

(These two schools, like many others, prepared an information sheet for teachers responding to job vacancies. They now also give them to new governors as an introduction to the school.)

GATEWAY PRIMARY SCHOOL

An introduction to the school

Location Gateway is a two form entry primary school in First Road on the outskirts of Anyborough. It has a pleasant three acre site and excellent facilities. The local education authority is Blankshire, which is fully comprehensive, and Gateway pupils move on at 11 to one of the seven comprehensive schools in Anyborough, the nearest being Broadlands.

The neighbourhood The school serves a mixed catchment area including the original village of Blackthorn plus a sizeable area of local authority housing of good quality, and a fairly new private housing estate ranging from starter homes to four-bedroom detached houses. The population is stable with little unemployment. Free school meals are provided for 11% of our children.

Facilities The school was built in the late 1960s. A nursery unit was added in 1977 and a new technology block in the last two years. The main building has 14 classrooms, a very large hall, and the usual administrative areas. We are lucky to have in addition a very large teaching space which used to be the infants' hall and is now used for music, dance and drama. There is an adequate hard play area and good playing fields. We have some rough fenced land for school pets, and a small pond.

The staff There are 15 teaching staff including the head and deputy (but not nursery staff), office staff, a welfare assistant, four classroom assistants and a schoolkeeper. We have curriculum leaders for maths, language, science, and technology. All age groups above Year 3 have some specialist teaching.

The children Excluding the nursery we have currently 404 on roll. No class has more than 30 but we are a little concerned that further housing is planned with, as yet, no plans for enlarging the school, though we do have space. The children's abilities cover the full range and the school has a very good reputation. We pride ourselves on the strength of our special needs provision and have a number of statemented children who are doing really well. Blankshire has a strong commitment to integration.

The governors The governing body plays a full part in school life and activity. Most of them live near the school and no fewer than seven are current or past parents. They take part in staff appointments on a rota and share all important decisions. Several come in regularly to help in classes and all observe classes at work, again on a rota. We link every governor to a class to give a focus to their work. This leaves five classes without an attached governor at any one time, but as the governors move up with their classes the effect is reduced to a minimum. We are fortunate always to have a governor from our local electronics firm ICON, which takes a great interest in the school, providing sports prizes and organising a Christmas card design competition, using the winning design for their own card. They provide a speaker on information technology for our parents and welcome older pupils to their plant.

The curriculum Obviously we teach all national curriculum subjects. Our chosen maths scheme is Factors which we adopted shortly after it was introduced in 1975. We are not dogmatic about reading schemes and use a combination of phonics, word recognition and the Guided Reading for Pleasure scheme which can be adapted to individual needs and teacher preference. The Literacy Hour has inevitably tended to produce a greater degree of uniformity which we do not altogether welcome: our standards before its introduction were very high and we still maintained variety and initiative. Music and drama are strong and we have no intention of reducing the time they occupy. All staff are trained in information technology and our children move on to secondary school with a good start.

Extra-curricular activities All normal primary school sports are played, football and basketball being most popular. We have a Pets' Club and clubs for Chess, Boffins, Art and Cookery. We will start a club for anything in demand, provided we have a staff leader or community volunteer. There are many curriculum-related trips and camping weekends for Years 4, 5 and 6. Parents' support is invaluable.

General The school is a happy place where high standards are not at the expense of the enjoyment of childhood. Individual differences are valued, and we try to build a warm and tolerant community.

Figure 6.2: Information about Gateway school

BROADLANDS COMPREHENSIVE SCHOOL

An introduction to the school

Location Broadlands is a six form entry 11–16 comprehensive school in Anyborough. It has an open site of some 17 acres. The system in Blankshire is fully comprehensive and the school draws on seven primary schools in the area. Students move on to a Sixth Form College two miles away.

The neighbourhood Anyborough is a town on the Steelville side of Blankshire. Its main source of employment used to be steel, but the closure of Platers changed it radically. Manufactures include clothing, biscuits, small electrical appliances and scientific instruments. The town is socially diverse, with several local authority estates and new private as well as older developments. There are reasonable employment opportunities and little serious poverty.

Facilities The school was built shortly after the Second World War and shows signs of its age. However, it has been well maintained and is light and pleasant. A new sports hall, library and music block have been added in recent years and the school is generally well equipped for its broad curriculum. Playing fields are extensive and the site is well blessed with trees and flowerbeds. We have four computer suites which are fully equipped. The library, with a full-time teacher-librarian, is a show-piece. We hope shortly to extend our dining hall and add an extra laboratory.

The staff There are 80 teaching and support staff including the head and two deputies. We are proud to record that all teachers teach their main subject and that there are no vacant posts. We have a good field for every advertised post and turnover is low. All teachers are graduates.

The students We have 960 on roll and this number is fairly stable. The school is always fully subscribed and some years, owing to successful appeals, we exceed our ideal numbers.

School organisation and curriculum The intake is split into eight tutor groups to give small classes in the first two years. Each form has a tutor and each year a year head to care for the students' welfare and general progress. Groups are rearranged for subject teaching in modern languages and science, where they are in sets according to ability in the subject concerned. English, maths, humanities, technology, PE, RE and art, music and drama are taught in tutor groups with mixed ability. In years 10 and 11 students are grouped according to their subject options and examination plans. All students receive personal and social education and careers education in their tutor groups, and work experience is available to all students in year 10. We teach all subjects of the national curriculum and in addition economics, business studies and Spanish. Children with special educational needs are catered for with skill and care, and we are very proud of the progress they make with us. We have a number of children whose difficulties are profound and in former times they would have been in special schools. They are very successfully integrated and we believe that they and their fellows benefit from integration policies.

The governors We have 16 governors including the headteacher. They all live in Anyborough and have varied and interesting lives in our local community. We are very proud of their commitment to the school and the part they play in its decisions and its life and activity. All those who have or have had children in this age group are Broadlands parents. They visit the school regularly and each one takes a special interest in some part of its curriculum. A governor always takes part in a staff appointment. We have two governors from local industry, who are very willing to share their expertise with us, currently one an accountant and one a production manager.

Extra-curricular activities Broadlands has a long and proud sporting record, and its rugby, hockey, football and netball teams play schools over a wide area and nearly always win. Other active clubs are gymnastics, drama, music, chess, computers, art and young linguists. Every teacher plays some part in out-of-school activities. We organise theatre and museum visits, history and geography excursions, outdoor activities camps and foreign exchanges.

General We like to think that this is a happy school where young people grow in independ-ence and confidence, make good relationships with their teachers and each other, and grow into hard-working adults who also enjoy life, make lasting friendships and respect people from all walks of life.

Figure 6.3: Information about Broadlands school

7
■ ■ ■

Building the Team

Since the governing body holds its responsibilities corporately, there is only one way governors can work, and that is together. This is a challenge for a group of assorted lay people, brought together it is true by a shared interest and commitment, but still with considerable scope for stresses in their relationship. Of course they elect a chair, but he or she only rules by consent. Fortunately most governors are now aware that good teamwork is essential and that self-discipline is necessary to achieve it.

The attitude of the headteacher is of prime importance. The headteacher who wants a strong and effective governing body can do a great deal to help the governors with their team-building, and will be rewarded by the quality of their work and decisions and their support and loyalty. Most headteachers have chosen to be members of the governing body, and in these cases they are entitled, as is any member, to suggest improvements in the way the governing body operates. Besides, heads are in a position to see the governors' work in perspective, and from this vantage point can often, if they wish, exercise a helpful influence.

This chapter looks at the characteristics of a good team and how these can be developed in the governing body. It discusses the role of the chair and of the part played by the various interest groups among the governors. It deals with the organisation of work, the observance of statutory rules and the acceptance of good working practices.

What makes a good team?

1. A good team has a common purpose and talks about it often

Why do people become governors? Governors tend to get very upset about their motives being doubted. What motivates governors? They don't have a simple aim like beating the next village at cricket or raising money for the

Third World, but when you spend time with them in training events, you soon sense the wealth of common culture and values they have. I could now tell after five minutes, if I were dropped from a helicopter, that it was a gathering of school governors and not shareholders or social workers.

The common culture This common culture has three elements. One has for many always been there – the warm feeling about education generally and a local school in particular which led them to become governors in the first place. The second is 'caught' rather than taught and comes directly from the time they spend with teachers. It is a blend of child-centred values shared by most people who work in education which governors have found infectious – I gave some examples in Chapter 1 when I talked about governors 'going native'. The third is something less easy to define but the most powerful of all. It is what ordinary and otherwise unconnected people feel when, for the first time in their lives, they experience responsibility for a shared and outstandingly worthwhile enterprise. I should like to see them more consciously aware of this almost palpable common culture themselves: firstly because any experience becomes more significant when you can put it in words, and secondly because they would know what it is they must cling to as a team.

Few ulterior motives In all those conferences I led on expectations referred to in Chapter 2 the sentiment 'to trust us and not doubt our motives' came in governors' first three among expectations of heads. It is hard it seems for others to believe that anybody could take on all that work without an ulterior motive, and indeed I have often heard heads say: 'We don't know where they are coming from' or: 'They must have private agendas'. No doubt there are a few who deserve that suspicion, but overwhelmingly I would say that governors give up their evenings, leave their homes and families, their TV and even half their supper to take part in something which is often frustrating because (a) they believe passionately in the importance of education; (b) they have a warm feeling about one school which has played some part in their lives; (c) they know, or find out on the way, that schools are addictively interesting places. Often they add: 'and besides, I felt I wanted to give something back'.

Shared aims need to be expressed Common motives and aims are the cement which binds people together and helps them to do what they have to do. They must have an opportunity to express the values which unite them. Otherwise they can get agenda-bound and make poor decisions. Heads can often create those opportunities. Sometimes a few well-chosen and well-timed words press the button which brings back the right associations. An occasional meeting to discuss issues rather than business can be liberating. Staff can invite a few governors representing the relevant committee to a brainstorm on a new policy on charging for out-of-school activities, say, a 'values' issue if ever there was one. Or you could arrange for governors to experience something which will remind them with tear-jerking suddenness why they got involved at all. It could be the achievements of a special needs group, the dress rehearsal rather than the play, the 1000 strong whole-school assembly when you won the European Panathlon.

2. A good team takes training and development seriously

Training on the agenda I touched in Chapter 2 on the expectations which governors should have of each other: a willingness to accept training and other developmental experiences is high on the list. Training should be on the agenda, and approached as a shared responsibility. (Training is often wasted if there is no chance for the group concerned to discuss how what was learned should change the way they work.) That means discussing their needs as a group, settling who's going to attend what and report back, deciding what they need to ask for that isn't currently on offer.

Getting to know the school The other developmental experiences, discussed in Chapter 6, include the process of familiarising oneself with the school at work. It is vital that governors, once they have settled on a realistic policy for school involvement rotas, take it seriously and are vigilant in maintaining it. You yourself, indeed, can ask governors to say in advance whether they hope to come to an event and write down who hopes to be there. Writing is a powerful instrument to those who don't do much of it and you wish to convey that you value their willingness to come. Then show when the day comes that you've noticed, and therefore that their presence is important to you.

Heads may need training too Remember that, if you are a governor, you can set a good example by going to some training yourself, since whatever your pedigree you may not have been trained to be a governor. Colleagues will really appreciate this.

3. A good team protects and develops weaker members

It should be part of the governing body's expectations that all will encourage the timid members and look after those who have problems of any kind, whether they arise from unfamiliarity with educational terms, from not having English as a first language, from general low self-esteem or from other real or imagined weaknesses. Other governors who may sometimes have a hard time are those who have a passion for 'doing things right' and can't resist stopping the action to correct procedural errors. If the errors are always trivial they may need joking out of it, but often they may get teased or worse for pointing out vital things we all ought to know, such as that if the governing body doesn't *elect* its representatives in a senior staff appointment, an exclusion or other appeal panel, it could be really dangerous for the school. (This is because in these cases a decision not properly made can be overturned by the courts or an appeal body.) If governors can be persuaded not to give this conscientious colleague a hard time all will gain. A governing body should not rely on one person to be its conscience.

Sometimes the ones who seem inhibited are parent- or teacher-governors having trouble with the representative part of their job, or even being told they are not representative (more of this later). Try to help them.

4. A good team knows the rules

Not knowing can be dangerous and divisive This seems almost too obvious to mention, yet many governors are not familiar enough with the working-together rules, and if heads are unable to help, very serious mistakes can be made. It *is* important to know, say, the answer to the question: 'Which needs the bigger quorum, setting the budget or co-opting a colleague?' Quite simple procedural errors can get an unlucky school into shaming and expensive trouble and a few such have reached the courts. It also happens that if some know the rules and some don't, you have all the conditions for power-drift: the ones who know move into the lead and the rest, knowing it doesn't feel right but not knowing 'where it says', stay silent and let bad things happen.

One LEA's technique Familiarity with rules is another thing governors should expect of each other. Northamptonshire LEA once asked me to write a pack for them called 'Working Together', designed to be used at all meetings to share rules and good practices. They gave it to every school and it was popularly known as the 'Ten Minute Rule Book' because the most popular way of using it was to give ten minutes of every meeting to reminding yourselves of just one rule, which was read out by the link governor, chair, clerk or volunteer, noted without debate, and reproduced in the minutes. With hindsight the LEA might say it would have been better to give the document in book form later to every new head and governor as well, since there was a danger of good habits lapsing when heads and governors moved on. A variant adopted by some schools was for the clerk to photocopy from the rule-book pages relevant to any agenda item and put them in the pack for the meeting. The rules don't change often (and when they do nobody rushes to summarise them) but they were revised in 1999, and I have given you Appendix IV which is a clear summary of the main rules operating since September of that year and slightly revised in the summer of 2000. Can you make use of that in your routines?

Preventing dirty tricks I have also appended to this chapter a few case studies illustrating various teamwork points (Worksheet 7.3). The issues are real – the circumstantial detail completely imaginary. A few of them show how ignorance of apparently dull and obscure rules can give dirty tricks a field day. Hundreds of questions I have been asked have convinced me that this is a neglected area of governors' work, and that we too often see rules as dull and bureaucratic, necessary but a job for another day, something we can leave to others, when in fact they protect our corporate power, our equal individual status, and many aspects of our honourable dealing. They stop powerful people becoming too powerful. And even a good decision, if improperly made, has the potential to get the school into expensive trouble. I am sorry to say that there are headteachers who couldn't pass a test on the rules without notice, and we do tend to turn to heads for guidance. This becomes doubly important now that schools manage so many important processes all on their own, and very few schools now have a clerk who is a fairly senior LEA officer (as most had when I began) to guide them when they are in doubt.

Confidentiality Some governors are uncertain about the confidentiality rules, and it may be necessary to remind them that almost all governors' business is open and that only they themselves as a group (not the chair, not the clerk, not the head) decide whether to classify an item confidential. Classification is clearly intended to protect the privacy of *individuals*, not to keep under wraps issues which are controversial or not yet decided: it shouldn't be over-used. Inexperienced governors may sometimes need to be counselled by the chair, however, that since they have privileged access to the school and are there so often they will pick up private things about teachers, children and families which it would be an abuse of their role to share. They may also need some guidance on reporting back, if they are parent- or teacher-governors, in a responsible way, confining themselves to decisions and arguments, not bringing in personalities or revealing who voted for what.

5. A good team accepts responsibility for its work

This means trying to keep ahead of events so that things get discussed before it is too late, dealt with elsewhere in the book. It means not blaming 'somebody' if things go wrong while you are day-dreaming, trying to remember what the rules said or wondering if you dare risk offending someone. It means talking about 'we', not 'they', even if you didn't agree or just sat there and let it happen. It means, in short, corporate responsibility.

Team-building is like gardening. There's always something that needs doing somewhere. This is because it's quite a difficult combination of corporate responsibility with individual equality: the moment the equality is threatened the corporate power gets unstable. Without constant attention power drift develops and the kind of malfunctions listed in Chapter 4 threaten. As in the garden, head and chair have to be ever watchful for what (or who!) needs staking, cutting back, nurturing – or talking to! *Remember always what was said in Chapter 4 – the best way to restrain the excessively powerful is often to build up the weak.*

6. The role of the chair

Sometimes it's the chair who is responsible for the governing body's problem, of course, and in this the head could be an unwitting accomplice. The governors may feel they'd like to elect somebody 'strong' so that they can sit back and watch. (Then after a while they don't like it.) A strong chair may suit the head very well, because he/she only has to establish a relationship with one person who'll keep the others in line. Often when heads say they are quite happy with their governing bodies, they mean that they get on reasonably well with the chair and that's really all that is needed. Unfortunately this doesn't always last, since the troops get restless, begin to drop out, and are hard to replace for the reasons given in Chapter 5. A mutinous governing body is no joke. It's particularly bad if they believe – whether or not it is true – that the head and chair sew everything up behind the scenes and the rest are just voting fodder. In any case schools have to make some very difficult decisions, particularly those that involve staff, and the governors' decisions will not be robust if there are some rumblings of non-involvement from those who see themselves as voting fodder. There may also be breaches of law, given that the chair has only very limited powers to act without explicit instructions. (See below.)

The chair: broad shoulder or team-builder? Ideally you will want both in your chair, but in practice you have to strike a delicate balance which may need adjustment from time to time. Of course you personally want a friendly and accessible human being to try ideas on, to explode to if you've had a bad week, to think aloud with. But the relationship should never be at the expense of other governors.

No special powers In education law the chair has no power to act without instructions from a meeting, except in an emergency – e.g. a fire or flood – so urgent that there isn't even time to call an extraordinary meeting, so serious that the school or any of its occupants are in danger. Even then the chair can only perform functions which governors would normally be allowed to delegate, and these are limited. This is not widely known, and many chairs are working from an old script. The result is that the law is breached somewhere every day. In most cases nothing happens, but it can be really dangerous if the decision in question matters personally to someone who has both strong motivation to go to the courts and a powerful backer like a teachers' union. This could happen over many personnel and finance issues or, occasionally, child discipline.

But even where there are no such dire possibilities it has a very bad effect on the team spirit of the governing body if there is any suspicion that decisions are sewn up or meetings manipulated in advance.

A good team player If the chair, on the other hand, as well as being a good listener, sounding board and wise adviser is first and foremost your ally in team-building, you have an ideal situation. Such a person will want, with your help, to bring out the best in every colleague, making more space for those who need it, intent on getting through the business but not at the expense of a good feeling at the end that nobody has been excluded. He or she will also be the one who from time to time brings the team back to what they are there for, and what matters most to them, creates a climate of high expectations and equality, gives a lead in supporting less confident members and corrects any tendency for individuals or groups to dominate.

The chair we deserve One rather sad thing is that the principle of 'unto him that hath shall be given' applies so often to the affairs of governing bodies. Take the relationship between a good team and a good chair. A good team is rather more likely to present you with a good chair than a poor one. A group of people who lack direction and breed inequalities and power struggles are liable to look for a saviour who will at a stroke solve their problems, and you may well get an undemocratic chair who will only further divide the team and restrict their development. A group who have already learnt a bit about good teamwork realise that, to build on what they have achieved, they need a leader with the same approach.

The time commitment Another irony of the same sort is that a chair who exceeds his or her legal role will have to put a lot of time into the job, and this will reduce the group's choice considerably because there are not many people who can devote that amount of time to it – remember there was a time when the chair was usually old or rich, and there wasn't even so much to do in those days. A group who are looking for a team-builder rather than a powerful leader who does not delegate will immediately have a much wider choice. Knowing that responsibility can be shared will make the time-commitment of the job seem more manageable. The consolation is that once such a group begin moving in the right direction they will soon come to see what sort of leader they want, so this will be a further reward for any team-building you can do as head. But is there a quicker route to a better chair?

Can I influence the choice? 'Can I more directly influence the choice of chair?' you may ask. Well, there is one idea which sometimes works. Try to persuade governors to get into the habit of using the first meeting of the school year to discuss issues relating to how they work together. Since September 1999 the regulations require all schools to review their committee membership and rules annually, and I believe governors could usefully extend this to anything which needs regular maintenance to stay healthy. This will put teamwork into the context. Then talk for a little while about the sort of chair colleagues want and the kind of relationship they would want with that person, before they actually elect.

Parent- and staff-governors

Some role confusion These are the only members of the team who have been directly elected and who therefore see themselves as having a well-defined constituency. Sometimes other members (and heads) imply that this is not significant, and that to be good members of the team they have to forget their constituency as soon as they arrive. This is a misunderstanding. New governors are often told that, in making decisions, they must always act first and foremost in the interests of the school as they see them, not those of any section of its community. This is perfectly correct, but to go on to say that they have no representative role is wrong, and arises from a confusion of the delegate role and the representative role.

I refer to 'teacher-governors' or 'support-staff governors' only in contexts not necessarily applicable to both. Otherwise the general comments referring to staff-governors in this section apply to both teacher-governors and the new support-staff governors elected after September 1999. In essence the issues are very similar for both groups, but as teacher-governors have been with us for 20 years and support-staff governors a relatively short time, there is a big difference in the amount of experience I have to go on.

Delegate or representative?

No-one on a governing body is a delegate, that is a member obliged to take prior instructions and vote according to the wishes of those who elected them. But there would be no point in the often time-consuming and expensive process of election if the products of it could have been picked out of a hat. What the representative status confers is a duty to listen to constituents, to convey their views to the governing body if they relate to its strategic responsibility, and to report back to their constituents on any matters not classified as confidential. In other words it is a communicating role. When it comes to deciding what line to take and how to vote, the conscience of the individuals and the interests of the school as they perceive them become paramount, even if in conflict with the views of the group the governor represents.

> *A vital role for the school No-one should deny the representative's right to communicate; all concerned should make it as easy as possible. It adds immensely to the effectiveness of the governing body and the acceptability of its decisions if it acts with maximum awareness of the views of the groups represented. That is the richness of the team.*

What can parent- and staff-governors take part in? The short answer is that parent-governors are no more restricted than any other governors. Neither are staff-governors, save in two respects: like others employed in the school (who sometimes serve as governors in other capacities), they may not be chair of the governing body or a statutory committee and may not be present when the pay or appraisal of an individual is discussed (though they can be on the relevant committee). But like all other governors, parent- and staff-governors do not take part in any decision from which they personally stand to benefit, where they have a conflict of interest, or where there are circumstances (like being the partner of a candidate for a job) which cast serious doubt on their ability to be impartial. A small builder, on the governing body as a parent-governor, would not, for instance, vote on the award of a contract for a building job which he might like to carry out. But he would not withdraw from a discussion affecting his child's class or teacher. A staff-governor is eligible to take part in selection of staff, but not if there is a candidate whose appointment might provide a vacancy for which he/she might apply. It is very bad for the team if members' roles are wrongfully restricted because of the group they represent, since it makes them second class governors.

Support-staff governors Non-teaching staff have not been represented for very long, most having been elected in the autumn term of 1999 under the provisions of the 1998 Act. Many schools (my own is one) have always used one of their co-options for an elected support-staff governor because they felt strongly that these members of the school team should have a voice, but now all schools other than the very smallest have a support-staff governor by law. Early days yet, but I have conducted a number of training sessions for the new members in a few LEAs, and have been dismayed to find how many had already been told (sometimes regrettably by the head, often by the chair) that they were not eligible to serve on any committees or selection panels, that they had to leave for confidential items, etc. I hope these misconceptions will soon be dispelled: they are full and equal governors.

Support-staff governors do indeed have a difficult job, because they represent such a variety of staff, in some cases working different hours and in different parts of the premises, and in large schools they may have to take more formal steps than other representative governors to ensure that they are aware of any concerns affecting particular sections. They may themselves, if their work is remote from the classroom, have some misconceptions about their role. They may not be clear about the nature of governing bodies' business, and may try to use the opportunity to bring up purely sectional and workplace-related concerns about hours, working practices, duties, etc. I have had to explain that the governing body is concerned in a broad sense with policies affecting the education of pupils, and although the welfare and contentment of all staff will undoubtedly involve issues quite properly covered by that description, there are other concerns more appropriate to line management, their union or a grievance process. In short it is not a works committee. I hope that more LEAs are looking at some specific training for these new governors.

Freedom to express opinions Teacher-governors have been on governing bodies for 20 years, but still they often don't play a part as full team members because, with or without justification, they feel inhibited by the presence of the head. Often they don't even know what the head thinks on an issue, but if it is controversial many will play safe. They know that their interests may depend on his or her goodwill. I am not suggesting that many heads deliberately engender this fear, but it is often there just the same. I have had letters through the TES column and statements at training sessions from teachers saying they have been carpeted next day for 'speaking out of turn' and even told that it won't do their careers any good. I would indeed say that because of fear, whether or not well-founded, teacher-governors fail to make the contribution to the governing body that they would like.

Staff-governors must play by the rules In fairness I must add, however, that braver teacher-governors over the years have sometimes damaged their cause by springing controversial comments on the governing body without warning the head in advance, or bringing up purely individual concerns of colleagues which are not policy matters. No doubt some new non-teaching staff-governors will do so too. I could not support these practices, and I always emphasise in my training sessions that it is one of the worst beginners' mistakes, and guaranteed to make any but a saintly head really angry. The head of the school is in an exposed position in a public body whose members mostly come from outside the institution, and it is very bad practice to drop him or her into a hostile discussion, especially one involving an individual staff member, without any chance to prepare. They sometimes do it because they are under pressure from colleagues to bring to light a matter on which there are strong feelings, and they fear being persuaded to drop it. They should stand their ground in the face of such persuasion, but never fail to let the head know their intentions in advance.

Staff-governors' vital contribution The confident heads who encourage staff-governors to speak freely, even on controversial matters after due warning, do a great service to the governing body. It would be splendid if all staff were able to feel confident that they would never suffer personally for speaking out on something of importance. Governing bodies benefit from teacher-governors especially being able to contribute without fear: they depend so much on them for informed input into discussions on the curriculum. It would also greatly improve the relationship between teachers and the governing body if teachers knew that their point of view was represented in the governing body's discussions. These considerations are more important than any embarrassment caused by the occasional ill-considered intervention.

The Taylor Committee indeed recommended that teachers in every school should have a consultative body which had independent right of access to the governing body with any serious concern, but this was one of the few recommendations that the government chose not to implement.

Parent-governors and 'constituency' concerns Parent-governors are rightly advised that they should not bring purely individual concerns to the governing body, reporting what has been said to them only if it has policy implications or significant numbers of parents are involved. What is wrong – and common – is to tell them that they should not even listen to individual concerns but refer them straight to the head. Parents rightly expect to be able to approach their representatives with a worry in the first instance, especially if unsure of their ground. Anyway it is in the school's interests that things get dealt with, by whatever route, and parent-governors may be able (a) to tell the parents on the spot from their experience that they've got the wrong end of the stick and perhaps explain the school's policy or (b) to encourage them to take the worry to the school and assure them that they will be well received or (c) to accompany them or relay their concern if they are really frightened of approaching the school. (If a governor does go to the school with the parent it should be made clear that he/she is not thereby implying that he/she has prejudged the matter in any way but is solely concerned to give that parent confidence to raise it.)

The difficulties of being a good representative I believe that many tensions on the governing body come from parent-governors' frustrated efforts to be good representatives, and where I have been asked to help in such cases I have often wished I could convince the head that establishing clear routines for hearing parents' worries – which the parents might fear were too trivial or based on misunderstanding – would actually reduce the volume of concerns, not cause it to grow. A weekly half-hour when anyone could come in without appointment, or a regular session with parent-governors, would take away much of the frustration.

Access to the agenda When parent-governors discover that any school policy or practice is causing concern more generally among parents, they should feel free to propose it as an agenda item for open discussion, and heads should not try to prevent this. But as with teacher-governors, it is vital that parent members are sensitive to the impropriety and folly of bypassing the head and bringing up new policy issues without warning at a governing body meeting, or wasting time with purely individual concerns. No professional should be exposed to such a situation.

The agenda

In theory the governing body as a whole determines its agenda, but in practice this is usually delegated to a small group of, say, chair, head and clerk. Individual governors who wish to add items have to propose them in advance to this group. If the request is refused, the governor concerned can appeal to the whole governing body, but to me this is far from satisfactory because no-one will have had time to prepare for discussion of it, it may overload the agenda, and the next meeting may be too late. I believe this is one of the few unsatisfactory things in the statutory procedures. Obviously every governor should have access to the agenda. Equally obviously in this case there have to be some safeguards operated by or on behalf of the whole governing body against items which are inappropriate, and also some means of keeping the business manageable. I think the solution would be for the DfEE to rule that any *three* governors can have an item on the agenda without question, provided they put it forward to whatever group the governing body has empowered by the proper date. After all three governors can legally call a special meeting. In the absence of such a change I can only plead that governing bodies should establish liberal policies to ensure that no governor is prevented from raising an appropriate item. This could be achieved by allowing any governor to add an item in advance without question, but make sure everyone understands that the whole governing body can disallow at the meeting anything they consider inappropriate.

Any other business Abuse of the AOB item must obviously be prevented. It is undesirable if a large number of matters are discussed without proper preparation, and some governing bodies refuse to allow such an item on the agenda at all. Indeed, some years ago I discovered that a county LEA had forbidden it in all its schools. I think this is wrong (and in the case of an LEA I doubt its legality). There must be some way of raising an urgent matter which couldn't have been foreseen, with the consent of the whole governing body. But I fully support restricting this to important items which can't wait for another meeting.

A word about committees

Committees and teamwork Chapter 8 deals with organising the work, but in the context of team-building I should like to say a word here about committees. In general governors are free to organise their work as they wish, but since September 1999 have had to have two statutory committees with special rules, one for staff dismissal and one for pupil discipline. These paragraphs do *not* apply to those, but only to governors' general committees on finance, curriculum, etc.

Committees that are well planned save work – if they are doubling it there is something wrong. Their membership must be consciously elected, should have a good spread of interest groups, and terms of reference and working rules should be clear. These matters must by law be reviewed annually.

Open committees? One of the best decisions we made in our school was to make these committees open. Our general non-statutory committees have a core elected membership, and those people guarantee to be there if they possibly can, and vote if it ever arises. But every governor is specifically welcomed to any committee and is informed about what is to be discussed. As a result we get an attendance averaging 50 per cent above the core membership, which gives more governors a chance to take part in detailed discussion. We also have a ready-made answer to anyone who tries to re-run a discussion in the full governing body – 'If you were so interested in the detail you could have gone to the committee.' Best of all, perhaps, the system creates trust. On that evening when you meant to go to a committee other than your own, you got home late, it was wet, and home was too enticing, the fact that you could have gone and know that other non-members will go is still very reassuring. You know there won't be any cabal-like behaviour, and that takes the pressure off. I must emphasise again that these paragraphs don't apply to the committees for which the regulations make special rules, namely those on staff dismissal and pupil discipline. Because of their role they may have only named members present.

Three worksheets are appended. Worksheet 7.1, a paper for discussion with your governors, asks 'Are you a good team?' and Worksheet 7.2, also for discussion, asks 'Was it a good meeting?' Worksheet 7.3 contains a few case studies built around teamwork.

I have already implied that the team-building task is never-ending, and it is certainly the case that members have to be vigilant all the time to spot signs of disunity, especially as the group changes its composition – even one new member can change the balance.

Everything the governing body does reflects its quality as a team. If it is a united team, with shared purposes, taking its development seriously, knowing and obeying the rules, sustaining all its members in equal partnership, behaving responsibly, it will be a great strength to the school. Every move it makes towards being a better team, apart from its primary purpose of promoting high standards for the school, will resound in its community, and make it a governing body people will be proud to join. Without great effort you as a head can have far more influence than you may have imagined, especially if you choose to be a member of the governing body. Your perspective on its work is unique, your understanding of what helps and hinders it profound, and your practical support in establishing the team on sound foundations could make all the difference between a group of mostly well-motivated but separate individuals doing their best, and a solid foundation for all that is best in the school.

Worksheet 7.1:

Is your governing body a good team?

Ask yourselves these questions about your governing body.

1 Do you feel that, even if they don't always agree about everything, your governing body are all there to improve the children's lives and learning?

2 Do you think everyone's contribution is valued?

3 Do governors talk often enough together about why they took this job on and what their priorities and values are?

4 Do governors all take training seriously? If as a group they feel that some members who need it don't go to training sessions, can they say so openly?

5 Do governors feel that work is shared sufficiently or do a few avoid it/hog it?

6 Do they have any agreed work-sharing rules or arrangements?

7 Do all governors spend time observing classes at work? Have they a system for ensuring that every governor does so regularly?

8 Do you all know the working together rules? Do you and your governors accept responsibility for good rule-keeping, or perhaps leave it to one governor who gets a reputation for being fussy?

9 Do new governors get a friendly and helpful induction?

10 Do your governors support colleagues who find it hard to contribute, try to find out why and give appropriate help?

11 Do they trust each other to be loyal and to keep promises about contributing?

12 Do they accept responsibility as a governing body for their own work, looking ahead, planning, and realising that they share that responsibility for what happens even if they sit there silent and let it happen?

13 Does your governing body resist any attempts to divide them?

If there are any questions you cannot answer affirmatively, is there anything you can do to improve matters?

Worksheet 7.2

Was it a good meeting?

Ask yourself these questions after your next meeting.

1 Were any new members or visitors welcomed and clearly introduced?
2 Did you have all the important papers in advance of the meeting?
3 Did your chair seem to have a clear plan for the meeting?
4 Did he/she seek agreement to any new agenda items or changes in the order?
5 Were you satisfied that the agenda contained all the items needing to be discussed at that time? Would every governor know how to get an item on the agenda?
6 Did members seem clear about the background to each item and the issues?
7 Did your chair set out clearly what the options were?
8 Were rambling or off-the-point contributions pleasantly curtailed?
9 Do you think all governors left the meeting feeling satisfied that the outcome was fair and without any sense that they had been prevented from having a say?
10 Were you as head treated courteously and asked to comment when appropriate?
11 Were you satisfied that you had been given the whole story and that the outcome had not been decided in advance?
12 If it didn't come to a vote, did your chair make certain everyone was happy with the decision?
13 Were you clear at the end what had been decided, who was to take action, by when, and how you would know it had been done?
14 Did the clerk clear the wording of the minutes with members on any matter where the wording was really crucial?
15 Were governors told about any important matters which would need their attention in the near future, so that they could be planning their involvement?
16 Did you feel that the meeting had moved things on in a helpful way?
17 Was it going to improve the learning of the children in the school?

Worksheet 7.3:
Three case studies

1. The plot that failed

Tall Trees Comprehensive served a mixed catchment area – one end university and professional, the other end poor. Traditional industries had disappeared, and recently established companies based on new technology (a) didn't employ many people and (b) couldn't absorb the largely semi-skilled labour force displaced from the former heavy industry. The school achieved some fantastic *individual* results – 10 As and the like – but overall the five A to C percentage only just topped the national average.

A great deal of conflict centred on the curriculum. The parent-governors, all from the more prosperous end of the city, resisted any attempt to 'dilute' the curriculum (Tall Trees had been a grammar school once). The staff and the LEA governors wanted to experiment with a more flexible options system to accommodate those who might do better with just five subjects; introducing short courses and more vocational options; starting popular new subjects like media studies and so on. The traditionalists started meeting in each others' houses, unknown to other governors, and produced their own proposal, carefully researched, to apply for specialist status and select 10 per cent of their intake. They believed that the way to get better results was to improve the intake, not dilute the curriculum.

The proposal was put to the governing body and fully discussed, though the chair administered a gentle reproof about divisive behaviour: nobody could believe that such a proposal could have been produced off the cuff or indeed without outside help (looking hard at a parent-governor who taught at the university's education campus). Still they were a good-natured lot. The proposal got fair consideration and was defeated. The head and the teacher and staff-governors voted against – they had other ideas for improving performance. The LEA governors were solid too – the authority was totally committed to the comprehensive principle. Two of the co-opted governors were against – they were from industry and said we should study how to get more leavers equipped for decent jobs, not how to increase the professor population! So it was defeated by 11 votes to 7.

Undeterred, the authors of the plan bided their time. They read their regulations. No, sorry, they read some of them. Well, one, anyway, the one about arranging a special meeting. Three of them signed a request for such a meeting, to be held on the first Monday of half-term. Only one item on the agenda, the consideration of a petition from a large number of parents about the school day starting and finishing times – it was a real issue, arising from the bus service from the old industrial area.

The chair's wife was a teacher in another school, so they were away for the week, and the (parent) vice-chair took the meeting. Of course the head and the teacher- and staff-governors were enjoying a break. Of the LEA members, who attended faithfully the normal governors' meetings which always took account of council meetings and were fixed well ahead, two could not manage this one. All five co-opted governors turned up because they happened to be from the area with the buses problem. Nobody was quite sure whether you needed the double quorum for the unannounced second item – it was a change in the status of the school, after all – but anyway they thought they'd manage two-thirds – and did. They reintroduced their specialist school/10 per cent selection proposal and got a comfortable majority of 8–5, two co-opted governors voting with the three LEA ones against, and one abstaining. So the way was clear to proceed with more detailed discussions.

Or was it? I said they hadn't read all the regulations, and it's clear they hadn't read regulation 35 of SI 1999/2163. After all, it's only three lines and a bit. It says that if a governing body wishes to rescind a decision made at a previous meeting, it must be a specific item on the agenda. In other words, nobody can get away with slipping in an item like that without warning those who might like to come that something important is coming up. So it was just as though that discussion on the first Monday of half-term had never happened. But what if nobody had known?

2. Too close for comfort

When new rules on exclusion hearings came into force in 1999, High Hollies Boys' Comprehensive chose the option of having a list of governors from whom the required panel of three would be chosen when needed, rather than a standing committee. They were glad the government had put in this option as an afterthought.

The boy facing permanent exclusion in this case, Simon Ross, was a disturbed thirteen year old, prone to sudden wild behaviour. Between whiles he could be sweet and co-operative, and he was not unpopular. Because of these unpredictable outbursts he was in danger of being wrongly suspected if no obvious culprit was found. Even on this occasion there was no clear evidence that he was the student who had thrown from behind some very corrosive chemical liquid at another boy's arm. There were a number of students fooling about, the victim hadn't seen his attacker and there had been no provocation or argument. No witness came forward apart from one boy who said he thought he'd seen someone who looked like Simon running away. Simon always reacted very badly under questioning, panicked and went to pieces, often cried, and so it was on this occasion. It looked bad for him. It was quite a serious injury, requiring a hospital stay, and painful. Simon made the case against himself much worse in his panic by saying that the victim was a horrible boy, a bully and a tormentor, and probably deserved it.

The chair of governors, Janet Hornsey, always liked to chair exclusion reviews if she was free, and she particularly wanted to do this one because she had said so often that Simon was a danger to others and she'd be glad to see him out of the school. She did tend to make up her mind before hearing the case, which worried some of her colleagues. In this case she shouldn't have served, because the victim's family were her next door neighbours and they were close. Janet, and her sister who lived with her, had been very upset to hear the injured boy crying in his bedroom at night, but nobody knew about this and she didn't volunteer it, so she chaired the committee. She was a forceful chair, and although the other two were uncomfortable about the flimsy evidence and also about the emotive nature of some teachers' comments about the boy, Janet's influence prevailed and they agreed to uphold the head's decision.

Simon's family took the case to an independent appeal committee. Simon also appeared before them. Following some new successful therapy he was now calm and rational, and of course maintained that he had had no reason to attack the other boy and indeed did not do so. But the things which probably swayed the panel – though we shall never know either that or whether Simon was guilty – were the evidence, the emotive tone of staff reports, and above all the possibility (which Simon's family made much of) that one governor's contribution was swayed by personal feelings and that she should have withdrawn on the ground that there were circumstances which made it difficult for her to be impartial. Their questioning also seemed to imply that they thought there had been some poor laboratory practice to have made such an incident possible at all and that the governors should have followed this up.

Simon's enforced return to High Hollies after an interval was painful for everybody, more so than if the challenge to the decision had come from governors. One unfavourable factor – the involvement of a governor who might not have been detached enough – could easily have been avoided.

3. A teacher-governor speaks out

St Saviour's was a happy primary school with a very talented head, Charlie Bright. He was full of new ideas and liked to try new forms of organisation. Some of his ideas were better than others but he always admitted mistakes when things hadn't worked out. But he wasn't good at taking criticism before he'd even tried a new idea.

It wasn't as though mixed age classes were altogether a new idea, though! Small village all-age schools had always had them – no choice. But St Saviour's was not a small school. Nor did it have the problem many schools had now of trying to keep infant classes within legal limits without a squeeze higher up. No, it was just one of Charlie's mad ideas. He was eloquent on the subject of how there was often more variation of attainment within age groups than between them. Besides, look how fast babies learned when there was already a toddler. What's more, he wanted to combine mixed ages with team teaching, which really got the staff going. No class or room to call your own? And what about the parents? It's well known they hate mixed ages. Nonsense said Charlie – our parents are really broad minded. But in his heart he hoped there wasn't too much discussion in the governing body because his parent-governors at least *were* very conservative.

Jenny Bold, the teacher-governor, had consulted all the staff conscientiously before the meeting. They were all horrified. She'd been well trained, and she knew she shouldn't spring her report on the head without warning him, so she went to his room and warned him, before she ran out of courage. But he had one of his excitable turns and forbade Jenny to make this report to the governors and stir things up. She promised she wouldn't say anything unless she was asked – that was as far as she would go, and even that was pandering to him. It was a teacher-governor's duty to report staff views after all.

Of course Jenny *was* asked. That lovely young parent-governor, Barbara, always asked her what the staff thought about things. So Jenny had to say that the staff didn't like the idea at all, though of course they'd do their best to make anything work. Charlie went almost purple. He was obviously going to explode. But it was the other parent-governor Frank who stole the show. He pretended he hadn't seen Charlie's face – he was lucky he had really thick glasses – and before another word was said he jumped in. 'We are so fortu-nate' he said 'to have a head who likes us all to speak our minds. I know of heads who won't even let their teacher-governors do their difficult job of reporting what the staff think' he said, 'but how sad that is when we depend on the teachers for so much of our knowledge. Barbara and I' he said, 'as parent-governors, we'll have to do our stuff now and sound out the parents, and I don't know what we'd do if we had a head who wouldn't listen to what they say.'

There was a long silence. You could have heard a pin drop. And what do you think Charlie did? He threw back his head and laughed. He's great, Charlie.

Note

These three case studies are entirely imaginary, the people and places fictitious. The issues they illustrate are real and I am sure many very similar events have taken place, perhaps known to readers if not to me. Please do believe in this case that any resemblances are wholly accidental.

Part Three

■ ■ ■

Working Together for a Successful School

8
■ ■ ■
Thinking with Governors

There is one thing which has scarcely altered at all in schools, despite the radical changes in the demands made upon them. That is the process by which they make their major decisions. It is a time-honoured ritual of thinking in turns, proposing and consenting, which worked fairly well in the days when few decisions made at school level were complex or had reverberations beyond the classroom.

In those days – say 15 years ago – the means to fund learning requirements, and the solutions to any problems which threatened the learning environment came from outside the school. The LEA had legal responsibility for the curriculum, fixed the staff complement and broad staffing structure, dealt with personnel problems and looked after the site and building. The school had a small amount of money per child to spend on books and paper and had no scope for changing its organisation very radically. It's true that most important decisions made at school level even then required the sanction of the governing body, but the nature of those decisions and the lack of wider repercussions made it rarely more than a formality. Only occasionally – as in the crisis over the William Tyndale schools in 1976 – did teachers' actions stray so far beyond the bounds of public acceptance that someone had to apply the brake, and even that crisis arose solely from issues concerning teaching styles and classroom practice.

But it isn't only local management of school finance, property, and staffing which has transformed the range and complexity of school decision-making. The pressure of a much more demanding public is encouraged by promises of school choice, entitlement to information, league tables and OFSTED reports. At the same time the government's pressure to raise standards is backed by savage sanctions, and the need to compete for various kinds of extra funding.

The governing body has been made by law an active partner in most school decisions and given ultimate responsibility for the most important ones. It could scarcely be otherwise when the source of alternative accountability, the LEA, now has only indirect influence. Professionals have to devise a way of enabling the governing body to make well-judged and robust decisions, satisfying the law and convincing teachers that those decisions are thoughtful and fair. Yet in most schools the time-honoured method of making major decisions remains largely unchanged: a process of propose and consent, bat and ball, to and fro, my turn, your turn. It is slow, problematic, and probably one of the most exhausting and frustrating aspects of a headteacher's job. The risk of making the wrong decision, or the right decision only grudgingly accepted and inadequately supported, is ever-present, and either way the penalty can be heavy.

I want in this chapter to illustrate the limitations of the classic process of making decisions, showing in more detail how inappropriately they serve present-day needs. I illustrate some of the dangers, and suggest an alternative which would involve better use of time, skills and varied viewpoints. This is not aimed at giving the governing body a more powerful role, and I accept that in most cases change and response to change will be initiated by senior management, with teachers fully involved. But some simple changes in the order in which things happen and the nature and timing of governors' involvement can create school management which is less stressful, more efficient, and in tune with modern needs.

How schools do their thinking now

Even the smallest school has some structure for staff to debate its problems and plans. The largest have a range of quite complex standing committees and working parties. They have routine work to do most of the time. Now and then, however, some new external requirement imposed on the school, some major problem that has emerged, or some innovative thinking by an individual, will call for a sustained programme of discussion. Then comes the bat-and-ball activity.

Starting point

A senior staff member has a brainwave. Or some intractable problem in the school gets so much worse that fresh thinking is necessary to produce a new policy. Possibly some change in the law or local circumstances is the trigger. Or an established school policy needs revisiting.

Consideration by staff

Whatever the cause, senior management embarks on a thorough examination of options and maybe their first thoughts are put into a discussion paper, either straight away or after reference to a working party or an existing committee. Perhaps one option is very costly and the possible ways of finding that sort of money have to be explored. Perhaps one will be seen as very threatening to staff. Another will upset the parents or the residents or a competing school. Anyway it's not going to be easy. There's no point in putting it to governors before the staff have seen it because the staff might throw it out and that would waste time. So the staff look at senior management's proposals and react to the various alternatives. Perhaps they add others.

Referral to the governing body

By now the head is tired. Do I have to do a paperback version? he wonders. He asks himself why everything has to be done twice. The big decision is how many options to put to the governing body, just one, just one with some tactical additions, or all those you considered? If you put in everything and it's 39 pages long some may not read it. Also, if you give too many options they may argue for hours, become indecisive and defer it or refer it to a small group. If it's very short and confines itself to a simple recommendation, they may ask why you didn't consider this or that alternative, why you didn't consult so-and-so. If you reply that you did indeed do all those things, they may be upset that they've been told half the story, and turn the whole thing down or refer it back for more information. If, on the other hand, most sit there expressionless while a few say what an excellent paper it was, and in the end it's approved without question, you don't know whether to be alarmed by such easy acceptance or offended that all that work wasn't even the subject of a few questions.

The truth is that it may be expecting too much of a diverse lay body to respond rationally to a complex, well written paper, a product of weeks or even months of talk, when it's the first indication they have had that there's anything afoot. There's no way in. Besides nice people are very reluctant to question anything in a paper representing such sustained effort by experienced professionals. They need to know what led to the issue being raised at all, what other possibilities were considered, why they were rejected, and what the teachers said. They need in fact to have been exposed to the issue and all its implications for all that time *you* were considering it, for any organic process of assimilation and reaction to have resulted. What you need is some way of giving them that experience directly, in fewer words.

Challenging times

What's happened to governors?

This time-consuming process is going on everywhere. Is it impossible to get it right? Tell them more, tell them less, what does it matter? Increasingly governors are grumbling that issues are only brought to them when the thinking is too advanced to change. They are also getting upset about being told half the truth *and* about being told too much; blamed by OFSTED for actions they had nothing to do with; held accountable for decisions never really shared with them; and expected to help gain parent and community acceptance for changes in which they may have no sense of ownership. Yes, governors have changed too. I'm sure the explanation is in part a system for involving them which is now threatening to buckle under its own weight.

Feelings of frustration may lead the governing body to resist agreeing too readily, and securing the necessary approval will be harder work. Even the most rational and sophisticated people who suspect that they are being taken for granted can react either by blocking decisions or having little commitment to decisions made. Their formal support, sometimes given because they haven't understood the paper or because they see no acceptable alternative to endorsing it, may then wilt under pressure, and these situations can be dangerous. Especially dangerous in my experience is a situation in which a complex but necessary decision alienates at least some staff. If the governors' support is rock-solid a head can survive it, but otherwise governors can so quickly join the mutiny or allow themselves to be divided, and that has turned into a full-blown crisis.

How have schools changed?

This is the real question – governors are simply reacting predictably to bigger changes. The decisions I am talking about, those requiring much consultation and thought, have become vastly more complex. Schools have taken on almost all the services formerly run by the LEA, so schools function in a dimension few heads have experience of. Schools can now, at extremes, buy and sell land and property, borrow on the security of their property, lend money, enter into contracts. Decisions about learning spill over into site and property management, personnel management, and now performance management. It's bizarre that while big business is busy farming out such expert functions, and new companies flourish delivering them, our non-expert schools are busy taking them on!

Difficult questions abound. If you reduced infant class sizes as the law requires – even if you have managed to do so without the dread vertical grouping which parents so hate – how much longer can you honour the god of choice and take all comers? If at secondary stage central government policies were to require a change in the balance of the curriculum, and this left you with a seriously wrong mix of staff, how would you choose between redundancies and an undesirably high proportion of teachers teaching their second subject, which would probably anger parents? And this on top of all the number crunching and the target setting, the home-school agreements and the codes of practice, the school organisation committees and the adjudicators. And the bidding, oh the bidding, for more special pockets of money than you can count, all involving evidence of this and costed plans for the other, outreach, matched funds. I am not saying it's all bad, but it's all such hard work, and it all involves so much decision-making beyond the educational.

The changes which took place in 1988 required schools to compete in the marketplace for the means to deliver a public service. That was the combined effect of tests, league tables, open enrolment and budgets based on bottoms on seats, sometimes laughingly referred to as payment by results. No, seriously, we didn't really need to wait for performance management to have the argument about payment by results did we? Not if you think about whole schools, rather than just teachers. We have it already.

Meanwhile governing bodies – those wizards in the ways of the world who were expected to help you – where are they? The pretending has to stop, now that they have been made responsible for school improvement in words no-one can misunderstand. Now all must have grasped what a few came painfully to understand when their schools were judged to be failing. How were we to know? was the cry. What did we have to compare it with? The original head in many of these cases will have gone, with the governing body left to plan the future. I expect some thought ruefully about how unreal some of their discussions were in the past, and how irrelevant, in the days when school decisions didn't matter so much.

The self-managing school Mark 2

One thing is certain: unless the head can gain well-based support, the school will be a lonelier place for some. I'm a great supporter of the self-managing school in itself – it has released vast reserves of energy and creativity, and opened prospects of more successful and exciting schools so far only dreamed of. I am sure, however, that decisions for the self-managing school Mark 2 require experience going far beyond that of the educator, overflowing as they do into the world of finance, property and personnel management, marketing, public relations and community affairs as never before.

> *No politician has ever proposed giving all that responsibility to one person because it simply wouldn't work. Yet we have not yet learnt how to make the sharing work either. The simple aim of this chapter is to remove one obstacle.*

If the Mark 2 self-managing school is to thrive it has to become in a new broader sense *a thinking school*. How can it manage the thinking and policy-making process? Not by thinking first and then consulting, perhaps needing to repeat the process as in my example, but by taking people's thinking along every step of the way. Easy to say, difficult to do. But stronger, safer, less tedious and even, in the long run, quicker.

Try first to see how laborious it is doing everything twice. When I talk to heads I realise that this is one of the things that makes them so tired. After the long process of brainstorming, researching, arguing for and against each option, deciding and disseminating undertaken by the head and nearest colleagues, the head alone, just when he/she is feeling drained, has to go and sell the whole thing to a group of people not yet warmed up to it, unfamiliar with the ideas and the vocabulary, and wanting to ask the questions you answered long ago.

Try instead to 'think governor' from the start

Imagine now how difficult it is for even able and successful people outside education to relate to the sort of highly-structured, closely reasoned document that appears before them without warning, how much more so for those who may have invaluable life-skills and experience not otherwise available to you, but don't yet understand schools.

A plan for sharing the thinking

Planning is the key to better decision-making with governing bodies. Since they do not necessarily know, unless you tell them, what problems lie ahead for the school or what issues will be coming up, you must have a means of regularly sharing with them what you see ahead. Then you can plan their involvement with them.

In the report almost all heads make to governors at each full meeting you have the means ready to hand.

The head's report as a planning tool

There are shining exceptions, but in general these reports do not make exciting reading. There is no special reason for the lowly status of such a potent planning tool; it is just how it has always been. Generally a new head will only have seen two models – one in the school he/she came from and the other his or her predecessor's in the new school. If the latter was dull there is a danger of further deterioration, since it will have aroused so little interest that the head wonders whether it is worth spending much precious time on. This moment of doubt may produce an even less interesting one and so on – a vicious downward spiral.

I discovered that a group of heads in an English county had sent an objection to the county's governor training team because governors had been asked to bring their last head's report, with a number of other working documents, to a training session. It is, of course, a document which anyone can come in from the street and see, apart from confidential items, so the trainers were bewildered. Nevertheless the heads saw the use of their reports for training purposes, out of context, as discourteous and threatening. But surely the significant thing is that they can't have been proud of them – if they had been they surely wouldn't have minded.

No participation in the past Traditionally the report has detailed the comings and goings of staff since the governors last met; what the children achieved inside the classroom and out; what outings they went on and what visitors they had. Nothing at all wrong with that, and we need it, but it has all already happened: there is no participation in the past.

Look to the future It could be a visionary document delivered in a bravura performance, expressing in addition the head's hopes and anxieties and a chance to look ahead creatively, guess at future needs, speculate. But this may not be your style, and in that case all it needs as a minimum is *a paragraph or two* flagging up things requiring action before the governors meet again, reminding them of deadlines, problems unsolved, ideas in the air, imperatives from many directions, and briefly describing the nature of the issue and the nature of the outcome required. It would be the sort of report commonplace in the boardrooms of the land, and it would turn the governors round painlessly 180 degrees to face the future. They could look at their meeting dates in relation to deadlines, set up a working party, begin to gather information, begin to think. They could fix up some representation on any staff bodies looking at the matter in question (more of that later) so that they would be tuned in to the brainstorming process, but always of course remembering that *decisions* must be corporate.

What kind of issues? Here are just some examples of the kind of issues I mean. Please don't let the list alarm you – it's just to illustrate the range from which about three or four items might come up in any one meeting. I repeat that it need just be a paragraph or two.

1 *From central government* – a change requiring a response from the school, e.g. a national curriculum change affecting primary school technology, secondary school options, etc.; yet another set of instruction on exclusions; a wide consultation on boys' achievement.

2 *From the LEA* – a rearrangement of catchment areas; a discussion paper on a further extension of budget delegation; notice of a meeting of a council working party on school building projects – a chance to put forward our music centre again if we're in time; new arrangements for local inspections.

3 *Other local changes* – industrial or housing development; population trends; influx of refugees from the latest trouble spot; a competing school deciding to go for specialist status; a new school being built in a neighbouring LEA.

4 *The world of educational debate* – a new theory on the teaching of reading; a book about some miraculous technique for behaviour management; a symposium on truancy.

5 *From our own school* – this should be the richest source, quite apart from the changing seasons and their needs. Is the character of our intake likely to change? The gender or ability mix? Are there trends to concern us in the age structure of the staff? How will reduced class sizes affect pressure on places? If school dinners get better will our dining hall be big enough? What happens to our timetabling when the extra large Year 8 with its huge surplus of boys hits Year 10? Should we look at the curriculum with a view to attracting more girls? Should we offer new maths teachers extra points?

Involvement of governors with staff in considering issues

Once the governing body knows what's on the horizon, the next step is to involve some members with any staff groups looking into any major issues on the list, i.e. important decisions with wide implications. All governors should in time have experience of representing the governing body in this informal role, but I cannot emphasise too strongly that it must be clear to both staff and governors that these observers are not there to participate in making decisions or approving them: only the governing body as a whole could do that. They are there so that a few members of the governing body are exposed from the outset to the complexities of the issue, understand the options and their repercussions, including their impact on staff, parents, community. They are soaking up those complexities. This does not mean that they can't contribute with questions or reminders about possible implications that may have been forgotten, but it does mean that they say nothing which commits the governing body or could be construed as favouring one or other outcome. The choice of governors on any particular subject will be dictated by which committees they are on, what form of link with the school they have (e.g. to a class or subject), their personal and professional interests and their availability, and they should keep their colleagues informed, under confidential classification where necessary.

When the consultation process within the school is complete, and the resulting paper comes to the governing body, it will not be a complete surprise to some of their number and some issues will have been reported informally to all. There will be some awareness of the reasons the matter came up, of its complex repercussions, of the questions asked, and of the implications of all the options. Apart from contributing to the more rapid and rational consideration of the proposals, this will help create the most important thing of all: trust.

It was interesting that in the new Statutory Instrument, the Education (School Government) (Terms of Reference) Regulations (SI 2000/2122), it was recommended that governors be involved with teachers at an earlier stage than at present in policy discussions. This was to make a reality of governors' strategic responsibility by ensuring that they were better informed about the matters they would later have to decide upon.

Teachers in governors' meetings

To achieve greater understanding it is also important for teachers to come into governing body meetings from time to time to talk to the governing body about their work, and especially this should apply to teachers who for any reason are especially involved in change. All round there needs to be more weaving together of governor talk and teacher talk if misunderstanding is to be avoided, and if both are to feel some ownership of decisions.

Snags

I don't underrate the difficulties associated with the changes I have suggested. The most common mentioned by heads is that in some circumstances staff have first to be acclimatised to certain new ideas. This is important, but the sacrifice of governors' early understanding of issues is a high price. I suspect that the purpose can be served by some small modifications of my suggestion.

Another objection is that heads and other senior staff may be afraid to show too much of their hand before they are sure where their thinking will lead. They may be even more worried about airing a problem too widely until they can see their way to delivering the solution. They may fear premature leak-ages to parents or pupils. But I suggest that the risks of becoming isolated by a governing body whose involvement in the decision has been too long delayed are far greater and must somehow be avoided.

An experiment with two very different termly meetings

I have already referred briefly to this but I need to say more because it is cen-tral to the subject of this chapter. Most governing bodies can no longer manage with just the one statutory meeting per term. Two is becoming the norm. Often it isn't because the business is too heavy: some schools with a good committee system and proper foresight can manage this with one. More often it's because governors need time for explanation and discussion of the issues behind the business and the implications for the future. An option worth trying is to have one business meeting and one 'issues' meeting a term, the latter also fixed well ahead and taken just as seriously, but often with more staff present and the agenda concentrating on the principles behind the business, on new problems arising in the school and on matters which will have to be considered soon. The discussion is still disciplined but more wide-ranging.

The advantages are obvious. Governors are better informed and have the raw material to plan more effectively. The gap between those working in or close to the education system and others is narrowed, as well as the gap between the more widely well-informed and others. Staff and governors have a forum within which they can build a better relationship. It lessens the dangers to unity and corporate responsibility inherent in small groups of the governing body going to staff policy meetings. Finally it informs and enriches the discussion of the business items to which the issues form the background. It can be a valuable adjunct to the other changes suggested above to make a reality of the governing body's strategic role.

The remainder of this chapter looks at some of the bread-and-butter aspects of managing the governing body's work.

Committees

I would not want to be prescriptive about what non-statutory committees a school needs, how often they should meet, etc. There are just a few general considerations that seem worth mentioning. If they work well committees should halve the work of the full governors' meeting, not double it! If you can achieve this they are a good idea because they allow more people to contribute, they facilitate a more detailed and less time-constrained discussion, and they improve governors' knowledge base.

Governing bodies should set them up with some formality because they are to a degree letting go of the responsibility they hold together and this should be a conscious act, even if it is a topic (e.g. the curriculum) on which no power of decision can be delegated, or one which they themselves choose not to delegate. Therefore it should be clear who the core members are and there should be clear terms of reference. Remember that a working party with a clear purpose and a time limit is also an option for a single issue.

All committees should report to the full governing body so minutes are necessary, though they can be simple (statutory committees, like the full governing body, may not be clerked by a member, but others may). It's sensible to have a logical sequence, ending with finance, leading up to each full meeting. Make sure you say clearly what you want from governors on any matter – to note, approve or give further guidance.

It's important that any committee has a well mixed group of governors. It shouldn't be too typecast – it's a bad sign if all the dark suits are on finance. Governors should feel they need experts to make decisions easier for them, not to take the decision-making over. All governors should believe that there's nothing intrinsically difficult about money matters. Parent- and teacher-governors should participate over the whole range of governor business as far as possible, and not be restricted by their role unless they stand to gain personally from a decision. The only legal restriction is that employees of the school may not be present when the pay or appraisal of an individual is being discussed.

Governors should understand about the necessity to have certain matters dealt with in a small group – anything in short which might give rise to an appeal – so that there are always enough governors who know nothing of the history to serve as an appeal panel. In practice this means naming at the beginning of the school year the standing appeal committees (on staff dismissal and pupil discipline) because of the need to assure enough members for first and appeal committees and keep them distinct.

Open committees? I referred in Chapter 7 (page 106) to our school's system of open committees (a fixed core membership but all governors welcome) which has increased attendance at committee meetings by about 50 per cent, built trust, and prevented issues being re-run at full meetings of the governing body. I think it is an excellent idea, and I can truthfully say that we have never had any problem of trust among us.

Governors' papers

One of the most vital aids to efficiency is proper paper management. I would regard the following as the points most needing to be made.

1   It is *essential* to store and catalogue agreed policies carefully, so that every governor can locate them and the governing body bring forward to check from time to time on need to update – new governors everywhere say that their greatest problem is not knowing what's already established policy and when it might be appropriate to put forward suggestions for change.

2   Governors should have some agreement what to do about papers which come to the chair but which don't necessarily need all governors' attention. There is a danger of a B team feeling if they are never mentioned, but few people want to see them all once they know how many there are! Good practice is to circulate a list, with action taken, at each meeting, but have the entire file on the table for anyone to look at.

3   It is good practice for all governors to see the draft minutes at the same time as the chair, with, say, a week to contest accuracy. This is not general practice in the world outside, but it is the government's ruling that minutes be made publicly available, with a clear indication that they are subject to governing body approval, once the chair has approved, and there is a growing tendency – which is good – to get the minutes out as soon as possible after the meeting. It seems wrong that governors other than the chair should have to wait longer to see the minutes than the general public, especially as it may be some time until the next meeting. It can still be made clear that they are subject to formal acceptance, and there is no need to circulate them again if there are no big changes.

4   It helps to encourage participation if now and then you ask a governor to take one agenda issue and present it, having done some preliminary work on it.

5   Tabling of papers may be necessary occasionally, for example if crucial information is late, but in general it is a bad habit. It impoverishes the discussion

and disadvantages governors who don't have English as a first language, don't read so fast, or need more time to digest unfamiliar concepts and words. You can't achieve perfect equality, but time and privacy do help.

6 All papers should be in simple and lively language and should carry an executive summary as well as an indication of whether they are for action, information or comment.

Conclusion

The first part of this chapter represents a major change in how the school organises its policy thinking and proceeds to decisions: I have called it 'thinking together' as distinct from 'thinking in turns'. It suggests that the head regularly sets out for governors the matters which will need decisions in the future, so that they may plan their information-gathering, consultations and discussions. It assumes that a few governors and school staff will discuss major changes and initiatives together in the formative stages of policy. Governors will thus be exposed to some of the exploratory thinking and understand better the reasons behind the proposals which will eventually be brought to them for decision. Such a change should dispose of the now prevalent – and divisive – view that governors are consulted only when the thinking has progressed too far for them to make any serious contribution. Its implications go far deeper than any procedures, however efficient.

I believe that such a change is now essential to:

- *demonstrate, by including governors in the formative thinking, that the governing body's legal responsibility for sanctioning major decisions is more than a formality;*

- *ensure that the school's decisions are robust, being well-based in knowledge and understanding, and taking account of the whole range of community concerns;*

- *increase governors' commitment to the proposals they formally endorse, thus making them more effective supporters of the school's policies and better ambassadors in the community;*

- *streamline the process of securing governors' approval.*

9
. . .

Better Communication

The scale of the problem

Language connects people. It also divides them.

Educators mostly communicate with each other, and their language has words and expressions not familiar to others. Acronyms abound and change frequently. It's tempting to indulge myself and produce a long spoof paper illustrating this problem but of course it's been done before. Anyway I don't want to advertise bad models. Yet a school in the average service span of one headteacher communicates with thousands of parents (some of whom find their own language hard enough) and a hundred or more governors, who come from all walks of life. Lack of a common language is serious when education has become the concern of all and when the law requires parents and governors to be consulted on many issues and governing bodies to make the strategic decisions.

Look at the prominence governors have given to their desire for plain language without jargon (see Worksheet 2.1 page 25). If we really believe that education is a partnership on behalf of the child we cannot ignore this problem, especially as, quite apart from the need to understand, language can give all sorts of messages which hinder and even sour communication. Also if we truly want to achieve a more productive relationship with governors we have to find the clearest and most accessible – as well as the shortest – means of sharing the issues on which we want their views.

It's not just the unfamiliar words but the concepts in which schools trade daily that need to be made clear. These form the basis of more and more issues on which the law requires schools to communicate with others. Much of my work involves trying to translate the provisions of education law into single syllables – not easy, because you have to be precise as well – and I find that this actually helps me to understand the meaning better myself. I think that in education we often slip into exchanging 'ideas' which are little more than packages of familiar jargon which clutter up real thought.

Forms of communication

Communication with governors

In your relationships with the governing body your communications will include regular reports at their meetings (*see also* Chapters 4 and 8); short statements seeking their agreement to an action proposed; and more ambitious consultation papers setting out the options in dealing with some problem or a change of policy.

Parents

Parents will receive notices of a purely practical nature and quite a range of statements required by law from you and your governors on the school's curriculum, rules, behaviour policies and achievements, with occasional need for explanation of some change of policy or practice. You will also probably help your governors with their annual report.

Golden rules

The golden rules for the language in both written and spoken forms of communication are the same:

- simple words, the smallest number that will do the job, and short sentences;
- minimum of jargon, spelling out the meaning of acronyms when first used;
- explanations of any unfamiliar terms or concepts;
- balanced selection of facts and arguments to focus on essentials;
- avoidance of words used unconsciously to establish status rather than to give information (we all do it sometimes);
- active, inclusive words in place of those that distance or exclude.

I say more later about 'inclusive' language. I apologise if this sounds a bit like teaching-your-grandmother but I have to say that I rarely read an education document, coming from any level in the system, from the smallest school to the Department for Education and Employment, which could pass all those tests, and the more knowledge people have, the harder, on the whole, they seem to find it to convey it to others. The trouble is that unless corrected our writing tends to get more jargon-ridden with time – and I'm sure I am no exception.

The choice of simple words needs no comment, and though technical jargon may be unavoidable sometimes, at least always translate it. Translations of complex processes or ideas take a bit more time and may even involve more words, though short ones (as in the first example below), but you will be rewarded. I am going to pluck some examples from a few papers I have read, and translate or suggest alternatives.

1 *'Norm rather than criterion referenced'* = 'giving exam grades based not on reaching a given standard but on the proportions expected to reach that standard. It could mean getting a better grade in a poor year for the same paper'.

2 *'Base-line assessment designed to facilitate the adoption of value-added comparisons'* = 'testing the knowledge and skills of all children starting school so that later you can compare schools by how much the same children have improved.'

3 *'With the object of bringing them into line with statutory requirements'* = 'to meet legal standards'.

4 *'Extrapolate from the audit of performance the principal results and implement an evaluation of the progress recorded'* = 'identify main strengths and weaknesses and measure improvement'.

5 *'Consideration is being given to the practicability of establishing an annual evaluation of the effects of setting on social relationships'* = 'We are thinking of looking every year at how putting children into groups by ability affects how they get on with each other.'

These are all real. The alternatives are not always shorter, but in these cases you'd have to wait a particularly long time on a street corner to find someone who understood the original words.

Inclusive language

Active and inclusive language makes a huge difference to the messages parents receive. It isn't just a matter of avoiding words which may not seem posh to you but which many people don't use in their daily lives. There are all sorts of tricks of construction as well as vocabulary, minor in themselves and rarely conscious, which separate their author from those addressed. It's well worthwhile invoking your governors' help, when drafting communications, to tap their community knowledge. If I hear of a primary school in a deprived area complain of uninterested parents (when a similar neighbour has them fully involved) I always look at some of their routine communications. They are often full of phrases like: 'May we draw your attention to ...' 'Your co-operation is requested ...' 'I am required to inform you ...' and 'It is anticipated that....'

There is a big difference between 'it is hoped' and 'we hope', between 'it would be much appreciated' and 'please', between 'it is a matter of considerable regret' and 'we are very sorry'. These are not just differences between complex and roundabout phrases and short ones. They are differences between the active and passive, the personal and impersonal, the direct and the indirect. This is better language for everybody, but remember also that there are many families for whom official-sounding communications – even typed communications of any kind – represent bad news, and if school news is good we want it to sound good.

Try asking your governors whether they think the school makes parents welcome. They'll probably say yes. Then ask them 'Does it make parents feel needed?' and they may hesitate. Language which includes the listener or reader in the sense illustrated above is a big help, though of course there's more to feeling needed than that! A school can make parents feel needed by willingness to communicate honestly with them about problems it hasn't solved, willingness to invite their comments on questions it can't answer. It can enlist parents' support for the child's learning in words which make that support seem like something special that professionals really need (and we are often told they do), not just an option for those with nothing better to do. In short the way a school communicates can make it seem human, fallible, dependent on its community, not self-sufficient and remote. You might look with your staff at a random selection of notes you have sent out to parents and decide whether with hindsight you could improve them.

More about governors' papers

Maybe there are heads who try to keep their governors in the dark. But they wouldn't be reading this guide. For the majority who are generous with information and very keen to keep governors informed, the point above about selecting the fundamental issues is crucial. The issues brought to governors are mostly straightforward, but everywhere they are drowning in paper, and the outcome suffers because only half is read. Also if the paper is unavoidably long make sure that you always say early on whether it is for action, comment or information, and that you include a brief summary of the arguments and the options at the end. Try not to *table* papers unless it is genuinely necessary. It puts governors on an unequal footing, and the most we can do to lessen the inevitable variations in their individual abilities and experience is to give those who need it time and privacy to read it twice, look words up, or ask a friend what something means.

I realise that often papers have to be produced at speed, and at first it may take longer to write succinctly than at length, especially if you also work hard at being relevant and accurate. The quality of the discussion and the decision will make it well worthwhile, however, and if working with governors is important to you, you will take a pride in it.

Your regular reports to the governing body

Much was said in Chapters 4 and 8 about the purpose and style of these reports, and especially about the importance of flagging up coming events and requirements, to encourage governors to plan their work. That is the report's main function, but of course all the time you will be increasing governors' knowledge of the school and their interest in it. Also, by giving chapter and verse to illustrate the school's achievements, you will extend their capacity to act as ambassadors in the community. All this will be enhanced by simple and lively language.

Don't forget to ask governors from time to time what other information they would like to have, and even when you have established a fairly standard format which everybody likes, don't be afraid to depart from it sometimes and give them a more personal insight into your feelings about the school and the events impinging on it, putting yourself a little further above the daily round. When I have seen such reports I have found the frankness and trust refreshing.

A bridge to the staffroom

One of the most neglected aspects of a governing body's work is the building of good relationships and understanding with the general body of staff. Even in schools where headteachers support governors' work in every other possible way, they rarely do much to influence the attitudes of their staff. Many teachers harbour strange misconceptions about the governors' role and some resent it.

As with most forms of institutional tension, better communication helps.

1   *Teacher-governors could do a great deal to improve communication between the governing body and the staff as a whole if they were sure of your approval, so make a point of reassuring them that you support this aspect of their work.*

2   *There is also scope for heads themselves to ensure that teachers are clearer about governors' role, about the constraints within which they work, and about the reasons, where not obvious, for their decisions. Remember that if you are a governor you must be loyal to corporate decisions – this rules out speaking to staff about the governing body in disparaging terms.*

3   *Direct communication may sometimes be appropriate, and I favour the chair or even the whole governing body talking to staff directly whenever they have made one of those occasional decisions which deeply affects them. Prime examples are an unavoidable redundancy; any other budget-enforced decision which adversely affects staff but which may have been the least damaging option; or reinstatement of an excluded pupil.*

4   *It goes without saying that governors' minutes and papers, where not classified, should be available to all staff; that teachers should regularly attend appropriate governors' meetings; and that teacher-governors should feel free to convey staff concerns to their fellow governors where these involve policy and are thus governors' responsibility.*

Governors' communication with parents

I am not now thinking of the formal communications imposed by law, but of the issue of 'visibility' dealt with in another context in Chapter 5. A good head will do everything possible to make governors' work visible to parents, since this:

- helps recruitment of governors;
- prepares parents for, and explains, changes in school policy or practice;
- helps to reduce complaints.

This last point may surprise those heads who seem to fear that the more you tell people the more fault they will find, and the more you welcome complaints the more you will get. I firmly believe that the opposite is true. Ill-informed mutterings and frustrated attempts to get heard can only multiply and deepen discontents. Put that way it seems a reasonable statement, but some schools do not live by it. My post is full of governors wanting to establish a 'surgery' – a poor word I know, since you don't go to the doctor to say how well you feel – and I know that heads often dislike it. But whatever you call it, it really is healthy to encourage comment.

I would also advocate the dreaded 'governors' surgery' (under a better name), with a clear brief that it was to discuss *general* issues suitable to governors, not individual concerns, and that it was combined with a half-hour session once a week when a senior member of staff would be available to deal with individual worries, however minor they may seem to others. I really believe that this *would* in time enable the school to respond to parent pressures effectively and courteously, and I have known cases where it has dramatically reduced the level of parent concerns expressed. It is almost always good to provide a structure where confrontations that won't go away can take place. But it is hard to convince heads once they have developed a defensive stance that they are fuelling the fires of discontent, not dousing them.

I know of a few cases where heads who have been really good in other respects have failed to cope with this kind of over-active community and its governors, and in the end have moved on for no other reason. That is very sad.

In many schools the governing body, or sometimes just the parent-governors, send out a short *newsletter to parents* after meetings. They would, of course, out of courtesy show it to the head first, and they would have to be content with the unreliable child post, but it would help to keep parents in touch with their work. The *agenda* is a public document, intended to encourage comment before the meeting, but only rarely is it placed on the parents' and staffroom noticeboards, which would be in the spirit of the law.

The annual report to parents

For five years I helped to organise and judge a competition for the best annual report to parents which was organised by the *Times Educational Supplement*.

Over the whole period we probably got less than 5 per cent of schools involved and even so some reports submitted were not worth a stamp. The general standard was high however and improved greatly over the five years, indeed at the end many were excellent and judging became harder.

The legal requirement to report to parents and meet them annually has had a bad press. I do not think many heads believe that it is worth much effort or money, and from time to time their representatives ask the government to abolish the procedure altogether. Moreover, while a number of LEAs encouraged their schools to enter the competition referred to, and took great pride in those commended, we discovered at the time that many others were encouraging schools to put the minimum of effort in and keep the format of the report on disc so that they could add the current facts and figures each year. They clearly don't expect parents to respond to such a document by turning up in person to discuss it, or think that it matters that they don't. Many heads share this view and argue for the abolition of the requirement, which I would consider very unwise. On the other hand, many governing bodies *do* take trouble to produce an interesting report and are very disappointed when few parents come to the meeting.

I would like to make a few points.

1   The report is important independently of the meeting, and a poor attendance should not be interpreted as evidence that the information is not valued.
2   Trouble taken to produce a report that is lively, attractive and informative will in time be rewarded – it does take a while for rights to be valued.
3   In any case it is good for governors to stand back and look at their work and evaluate it and to see the school in perspective.
4   It is a good exercise in teamwork, ideally planned and co-ordinated by a small editorial group but with contributions by many hands.
5   The legal information can be appended, giving the governors freedom to make the rest a good brisk read.
6   The report should deal particularly with matters of special interest to parents – the health and welfare of their children, social and sex education, fun activities, behaviour, as well as academic matters.
7   It should clearly be a *governors'* report, written in homely language and with a different perspective from other school publications.
8   Above all, it should deal with matters that invite parental response, which means the future and not just the past – the unsolved problem, the burning issue, the next bit of thinking – and encourage parents to give their views.
9   In total, parents should feel *needed*, not just welcome.

The meeting depends on the report more than anything else, especially the last two points above. Nevertheless many schools have successfully linked it to another event, and anything in which the children participate is an obvious draw. I have discovered two tips that seem to work. One is a reminder three days before – especially if it comes from the parents' own association and is freed from the legal language few invitations escape. Bear in mind that, while some people have diaries going months ahead, many people don't. Another tip is to organise the first half of the meeting around café style tables with a governor, a few reports and something to drink on each. A chance to warm up in a small group often produces more questions in plenary session.

Don't over-do the 'quorum' issue. It's not right to call it a quorum first of all. The 20 per cent requirement applies only to formal resolutions guaranteed a response. It may be a perfectly good meeting with less than 20 per cent, counter-productive to discourage those who have come for the sake of those who haven't, and a bonus if there's a real issue to discuss. I once attended a meeting at a primary school where the head tried to obstruct discussion of a very serious, thoughtful and important matter raised by 70 parents because 20 per cent would require 89 signatures. He wasn't successful.

Conclusion

The headteacher is at the hub of the school's communication system, and can initiate, encourage and improve the messages that are exchanged between groups with great benefit to relationships. Some heads like to have one person check all written communications that go out for correctness and consistency – this is understandable, especially in a very large school where many people send out bread-and-butter messages about coursework, football fixtures, payment for trips, clubs, and some will be more polished than others. But a school should surely not aim for every communication to have a recognisable identity, or value conformity at the expense of spontaneity. The really important thing is that all messages convey to those who receive them that they are valued by the writer as partners in education, and that language never becomes a barrier.

10
■ ■ ■

Raising Standards

This chapter is about school improvement, a phrase which occurs in almost everything now written about schools. Since the Schools Act of 1992, which established the Office for Standards in Education (OFSTED) and its national programme of school inspections, and the 1993 Act which outlined the 'special measures' regime for schools found wanting, school improvement has been the foundation of education policy and practice.

A change of government certainly made little difference: indeed the theme became stronger than ever in the 1997 Act which straddled the General Election and was agreed by the two front benches. That Act established base-line testing and first introduced statutory behaviour policies and home-school agreements, these latter provisions repeated in the School Standards and Framework Act of 1998. In that Act almost every major provision is related to school improvement, as you will see from the summary in Appendix II. To this end it provided for:

- *class size reductions in the infants stage;*
- *LEA development plans to raise standards;*
- *a new duty on governing bodies to promote high standards of achievement;*
- *education action zones;*
- *a strong focus on discipline, with behaviour guidelines, home-school agreements and attendance targets;*
- *stronger measures for failing schools.*

The involvement of governing bodies

Responsibility for the improvement process

Governors are deeply involved in all these provisions. It is the governing body which has to draw up action plans after OFSTED and report regularly to parents on progress in implementing those plans. The governing body produces the behaviour policy and the home-school agreement, sets targets for school performance and attendance, while the general statement of the governing body's primary function spells out for the first time a duty to conduct the school in such a way as to improve its standards.

Furthermore the briefings given to OFSTED inspectors included, not long after the inspections were established, a requirement to include in their investigation the extent to which governing bodies were carrying out their responsibilities and their involvement in the school generally. This change produced a crop of reports in which the governing body was found wanting, and incidentally anger among some governors who felt that they had never been given an opportunity to get involved in the matters on which their performance was criticised. More than a few heads whose schools had escaped such a criticism will have said 'There but for the grace of God ...'.

When governors have been found wanting

Following this first crop of critical reports, the heads and governors of several schools where the governing body had been criticised invited me to visit them to try to help them towards a more appropriate level of involvement. Naturally the heads concerned were as disturbed as the governors and just as anxious to avoid any further criticism. We went through their working practices, concentrating particularly on their awareness of their role, their access to strategic information, their familiarity with the school at work, their teamwork and relationships. But from wider contacts I know that these governors and their heads were the unlucky ones. In many schools I know which have so far escaped criticism there is just no relationship within which governing bodies can assume their legal role. Indeed, in the schools I have in mind such a consultation with an outsider would never have been accepted by heads deeply resistant to any form of open governance.

I will not attempt to apportion blame for this between inadequate and apathetic governors on the one hand and resistant heads on the other: that doesn't move us forward. I only know that more able and highly motivated local people will only come forward as governors if there is a real job to do, and it is, in the main, the heads who have the power to change this. Not only do they have the power: they have much to gain from using it.

School improvement as a continuous process

I think most people believe as I do that improving a school needs more than a short series of dramatic and well-publicised changes and a few deft cosmetic touches, and are sceptical when they hear about schools that have been 'turned around' in what seems a very short time. I would think it takes a school a long time to plan really significant changes, get them accepted, back them up with good working practices and embed them organically in its work and in the life of the school community. The acceptance in particular is crucial and not always easy to secure.

All duties well performed make a contribution

One can always encourage governing bodies who feel helpless to effect any improvement by pointing out how big a contribution the efficient execution of their 'old' jobs makes. Sometimes they don't see any connection; sometimes they feel overawed by the more specific school improvement measures they hear about. So, for instance, they can be assured that children's learning is clearly advanced by:

- wise and careful spending of the school budget;
- choice of first-class senior staff to give leadership;
- a safe, healthy and stimulating environment;
- good personnel practice, and decisions affecting staff which are based on open and consistent criteria, so vital to good morale;
- clear and fair guidelines for behaviour management, and again decisions affecting individual children which are transparently fair;
- friendly contact with the school at work, learning about the curriculum and sharing teachers' enthusiasms.

In addition, of course, rising standards depend on sound policies in all areas of governors' responsibility.

These factors may seem obvious, and of course we must move on to more specific approaches to academic standards, but when governors feel over-whelmed by the magnitude of the injunction 'to improve the school' it can be very salutary to point out the contribution to quality learning which their familiar tasks already make. Most governing bodies could improve the way they carry out these general responsibilities, and believing that this contributes to school improvement is a big incentive. They also need reminding (and all governor trainers will say 'Amen' to this) that there is no 'quick fix' which will enable them to tackle the specifics of target setting and monitoring unless they have established the basics. These are:

- role clarity;
- corporate responsibility;
- involvement in the life of the school;
- good teamwork;
- effective execution of their duties.

On these the performance of all other duties depends. Chapters 3, 4, 6 and 7 all have a bearing.

More specific approaches to school improvement

This is where governors begin to feel inadequate and ring up their training team for the 'quick fix', some worksheet or other form of instant illumination. They have always been hesitant about venturing into professional territory and what used to be called the secret garden of the curriculum. They know that, in order to make any direct impact on the school's standards, they need to know a great deal more about what goes on in that secret garden; have much more specific information about how the school performs in tests and examinations; and have additional information which will enable them to judge that performance in context, which means data on pupils' starting points and comparative information on other schools. It is the headteacher's duty to see that they receive this information.

Now is the time to look at the governing body's curriculum committee or working party, where the detailed work on performance should be initiated. This above all should be an active and representative group, which as well as studying the data mentioned should be familiarising itself with the school curriculum, always having a curriculum leader on a particular area of work to each meeting to talk about that work. This not only provides valuable background material regularly updated, but makes it easier to delve a little more deeply, when any curriculum area is causing concern, without making a big deal of it.

New sensitivities

In fairness to governors, some teachers and heads don't make access to the secret garden all that easy. Governors tell me there have been reactions, to target-setting in particular, so strong that you would think governors had only just been invented. We've all been rummaging for those things from the tool-shed mentioned in the Introduction, things to oil relationships, mend breakages, tighten up procedures and replace blown fuses! Heads have a big responsibility to keep things calm and remind teachers what government policies require. It doesn't warrant a massacre of the messengers!

Professional resistance may also hold up more detailed information on school performance, without which the target-setting exercise can be meaningless anyway. Some teachers seem to hate turning their hopes into percentages even privately, much less in public, so suddenly having to do that *and* having outsiders trying to get a point or two more out of them was hard. Even more painful is the moment a year on, just about the time I write this, when perhaps some of the first targets have not been met and heads, teachers and governors have to face this together.

Finding a level playing field

The speed with which many governing bodies have understood and publicised among parents the pitfalls of raw test scores is amazing. They all know that the playing field is not level and why, and are looking for and increasingly finding statistics which adjust the figures for their school's circumstances. This is healthy, and without the hated raw statistics and their legally enforced publication, I do not think that that necessary process would have advanced anything like so fast. The information is improving all the time. I hear quite often of governors who do not see the PANDA (Performance and Assessment) reports, and I don't know why, but all heads should watch this. I believe that each governor should get individually from the LEA these excellent local reports on school performance, which put this performance in context.

But don't forget that these same advances also reveal differences between schools and teachers more cruelly than some of the crude comparisons they were designed to replace. At least the crude comparisons carried their own excuses and at least they covered up a lot of the revealing detail. In the days of the raw figures it was easy to blame the intake, but now fairer comparisons not only of schools but also of individual teachers can sometimes be made. We have a lot of growing up to do. Nevertheless schools must identify and tackle weaknesses, and if it is to mean anything, governors must not only be fully informed, but also mature sufficiently in their role to be able to identify themselves with the school, happily with its successes, painfully with its weaknesses. When governors say 'we', they must really mean it.

What governors should look for

One of the hardest tasks for both heads and governing bodies is to identify the strategic information the governing body needs to make any contribution to improved performance. That is perhaps even harder than helping them to identify the knobs and levers which can alter for the better the conditions in which teachers do their work. Harder because, if you don't know what there is, you don't know what to ask for, and heads have to win governors' total trust when they are the only sources of such crucial selection. Certainly governors need to understand the application of value-added in all its forms – the principle is easy but the maths rather hard – and in addition I always urge them to bear six basic suggestions in mind.

1 Remember that you are looking at the performance trends of *all* the pupils, not just the headline figure. That means the very able and those with special educational needs and all those between. It means in secondary schools those who get one GCSE pass as well as those with 5 grades A to C (an exam designed for everybody, remember) and in particular look at those who, with enormous effort, manage passes in English and maths – remember employers value these, and even very modest GCSE passes carry entitlement to some popular courses at 16+.

2   Everything that happens in the school is relevant – sports and clubs as well as classroom subjects. It is all education – if not, why is a school doing it? So look at the number and range of, and participation rates in, out-of-class activities, and consider what improvements are possible.

3   Try to understand all the value-added calculations and their significance, since they show how the school has helped children of different abilities to progress.

4   Give particular attention to differences in the performance of various groups based on e.g. gender, home circumstances, time of year born, attendance record, and try to identify the nature and extent of the differences and possible reasons.

5   Remember that improvements are rarely a straight upward line – they jump up and down with different intakes, but over time progress should be discernible.

6   Share what you have learnt with parents you encounter – it's part of your job to help *them* to understand how the school is doing.

I hope that this guidance will also help steer heads to the most useful selection of data for the governing body.

Knobs and levers

Once the governing body have the necessary material to participate in your improvement programme they need to be doubly aware of all that was said in Chapter 3 about roles and boundaries. They need to understand that 'strategic' doesn't mean observing teachers and helping them to teach better. *This remains true even now you know a lot more about the school's performance.* Direct measures aimed at improving teaching are the head's or adviser/inspector's job. Nor does it mean precipitating teachers into in-service training or, *in extremis*, competency procedures. It means learning what factors can improve performance from the governing body's strategic distance, and they are many. Choice of syllabus or exam board, size and ability mix of teaching groups, personnel and pay policies, and above all how you select, train, use and direct curriculum leaders and departmental heads (middle management). Non-contact time may be a relevant factor here and this brings in wide-ranging issues of school organisation. I am as anxious as any head to direct governors' attention away from operational issues, but you must play your part by sharing genuinely strategic information and helping the governing body to use it.

Governing bodies and OFSTED

Preparing for the inspection It is in the run-up to the inspection that the part governors can play is often underrated. Heads and staff are very tense and governors can do much to raise morale and put the inspection in perspective. In particular it helps enormously if governors can remind teachers of the things the school does outstandingly well. There is a tendency – perhaps the fault is in the process itself and its political overtones at the time – for them to be obsessed with the things they haven't done or do less well, and temporarily their confidence in themselves and the school is damaged. I have known governing bodies work wonders in this situation, emphasising the school's strengths and putting its shortcomings in proper balance in all their contacts with staff.

Policy-writing mania The frenzy that overcame schools in the first round of OFSTED inspections was, of course, about policy-writing. All concerned were well aware that the school was obliged to have a number of written policies ready for inspection and few schools were confident that they had done all they should. So there followed a scramble to get policies written. Probably much that was written for that purpose never again saw the light of day, and didn't bear, and had never borne, any resemblance to what actually went on in the school. Useless to try to persuade staff or governors that inspectors were well able to smell midnight oil and new paper, and would give far more credit to honest work in progress on an issue. Useless to say that few schools would have done everything, and that inspectors were not looking primarily for such things. The second round seems to have been calmer.

During the inspection I have been surprised how much schools vary in their policies on involving governors in the inspection. At one extreme they will, unless the inspectors insist, confine pre-inspection contact to the chair at most. At the other, inspectors will as a matter of course talk to the whole governing body beforehand and consult governors with particular responsibilities, e.g. the SEN governor or the chair of the finance committee, as and when they need to. Obviously this all has to do with confidence and trust. I wouldn't favour governor presence during the inspection, which is so brief, intensive and, for many, stressful, but I certainly think they can be of help in briefing inspectors and by being available for informal consultation when needed. They know a great deal about the community served by the school, and this, they sometimes complain, inspectors too hastily classify. They must also have an opportunity to talk directly to inspectors about their own role and how they fulfil it: the inspectors are required to report on this and their findings should draw on what the governors themselves say. Well-informed and loyal governors can do the school nothing but good during this time. At least the report back at the end is normally full and informative, and made to the whole governing body.

The long haul The legal responsibility for issuing an action plan and monitoring its implementation is beyond any doubt the governing body's, and some have had little experience of such tasks. They lean on the professionals to translate statement into plan. Even so some plans I have seen do little more than repeat, in the form of intentions, the key points made in the report. This

143

can produce 'plans' with no process content like 'Improve differentiation in maths teaching' or 'Diversify Key Stage 4 curriculum' or 'Pay more attention to formal grammar in modem languages'. Governors do need teachers' help to formulate plans which mean something, but this is no reason why their involvement should be a sham. They can ask searching questions, choose between alternative strategies, and argue, where targets seem too timid, for shortening the time-scale. There should always be a firm programme for reviewing progress, not a hasty fudge just before the annual parents' meeting. Governors can be immensely valuable in interpreting the report for parents and putting in context any points that might otherwise be misleading.

To sum up The OFSTED experience is, of course, a prime potential source of border incidents between governors and staff, especially as everyone is nervous. On the other hand, the inspection process produces one of the most interesting tests for the partnership, where strategy meets daily performance; where a bird's eye view swoops down to detail; where detached reassurance confronts institutional stress; and where commitment to improve meets cautious detail in a plan to achieve it. Above all, it brings governors to a sharp realisation of their responsibilities to interpret the school to its parents and neighbourhood. They should learn a great deal from the experience.

'The patient is making good progress'

This isn't about crisis management and disaster limitation, though it *is* about schools which are suffering or recovering from a testing experience. It may be a bad OFSTED report which introduced the dread 'special measures'. It may be the loss of a headteacher owing to health failure, misdemeanour or simply burn-out, all of which cast shadows behind and before. Most commonly in my own experience it is the implementation of a change so radical that it causes deep conflict between head and staff. My concern is how a governing body reacts to such a challenge and the part it can play. My best experiences have been where a governing body has been solidly behind the head in what he/she wants to achieve, and have so sustained and re-energised him or her through the trauma that bonds have become strong or been reinforced.

A story of the failing school that won a prize

I spoke earlier about the TES competition for the best annual report to parents. In its fifth year the judges awarded a prize to a failing school in a little village in the heart of the countryside on the border between England and Wales. Everybody who handled the entry, in its progress from a big sack among several sacks to the judges' table, wanted it to win, and these were experienced trainers who sifted the large entry and classified those with merit. I suspect that some judges from outside the governor fraternity may have raised their eyebrows at the thought of honouring a failing school. But they agreed in the end that they were judging a piece of communication, not inspecting a school, and as such it was superb.

The chair came to London to receive the award. To start with it was a familiar story: 'How were we to know? It's the only school in the village, the teachers worked hard, the children loved going to school and seemed to be getting on. We weren't much involved. What did we have to compare ourselves with? How could we judge?' From that point it got a bit more special. Honesty. Total honesty. The letter with the full story went not just to parents but to every household in the village. 'It is our village school. They must be told everything. And they must be told what they can do to help. From now on it's hard work and uphill all the way.' The story was told again simply, but very movingly, in the annual report to parents, for by this time the uphill road had an end in sight. Local inspectors were amazed at the pace of change, the community spirit. The comments of the original inspectors on the school's deficiencies as a place of learning had all been taken seriously, but so had the very bad condition of the building which was a symbol of its demoralisation. Many people helped and a local firm donated a number of days' free labour to break the back of it.

The governing body provided leadership until a new head took office. They tackled staff problems, curriculum planning and reformed organisation. They had learnt such a lot and would never be the same again. This was a moving experience which demonstrated both governors' inability still, in many school situations, to avoid catastrophe, and their amazing capacity to respond to it. This is the only failing school I have had personal communication with, but I am sure that many other governors have experienced both the limitations and the scope of their role in similar circumstances.

That was a story of shock and dismay, on a par with a death or a natural disaster for rocking a school to its foundations. We are talking about ordinary people in extraordinary situations. What I want to do now is to look at more common situations which are not of headline proportions but which illuminate the potential of the head/governing body partnership and show how it can grow and help schools grow.

Major reorganisations

Many heads, new or with new insights, find the organisation they have inherited out of harmony with their ambitions for an improving school. It may be top-heavy. It may have weak middle management. It may be inadequate on the pastoral side or insufficiently rigorous academically. In a primary school it may, in its determination to improve numeracy and literacy, have missed the stretching of the imagination, the development of manual skills, the flowers that grow beyond the paths. A comprehensive may have too little provision for the less academic at Key Stage 4. It may on the other hand have inadequate challenge for the very able. All these perceived imbalances mean big upheavals for many people, possibly redundancies. However gradually plans are implemented they will produce stress and fear.

Sharing plans A wise head will ensure that priority is given to sharing concerns with the governing body. They may be shocked at first by the prospect of so much upheaval, but one thing is sure: staff and parents are going to be even more shocked, and the head needs allies. Often these heads are surprised to find how easily they strike sympathetic chords. Governors may not have been able to see the whole picture, but they are unlikely to fail to recognise the individual problems as such when these are set out before them. They may even have been longing for someone to say what they had long suspected.

Sharing the action When an opportunity comes to turn the plan into action, in whole or in part, the governing body are essential. They give it status, weight and often indeed legality. I have found that their role is particularly important when the head's resolve momentarily flags: he or she may not be able to face arousing any more hostility among the staff. Governors may see more clearly that the hostility won't melt away even if the plan is aborted, and the real danger is that the head will have the worst of all worlds, a disaffected staff and nothing to show for it. Often a head will find at this stage that sharing the problems from the beginning has made all the difference.

Picking up the pieces Even when there is no turning back the tiniest slip can be dangerous. If someone is to be without a job at the end, governors can even worry about little things like the sun coming round the building as the interviews wear on and being in a later candidate's eyes. I have observed a few governing bodies through such traumas and I have to say they have shown qualities that even an optimist like me could not have predicted. Just as when difficult budget choices have to be made, a governing body which feels some ownership of a decision seems to be able to hold on tight to the reasons for it and the benefits hoped for. But the schools I am thinking about now have all been ones where governors have been valued and trusted, and this has given them the strength to carry on through the hard times. That is the key.

Conclusion

School improvement, whether a continuous process or a major upheaval, involves difficult choices and hard decisions. With the informed support of a concerned but detached body of people these can be a great deal easier. In training sessions with governors I often give them my patent cure for being too nice. It is to shut their eyes and think about the children. Not to think of them lining up or singing a hymn or quietly doing their work, but doing some of the many touching things a visitor notices, white knuckles clasped around a recorder, tongue in the corner of the mouth doing the first bit of joined-up writing, gangly squeaky adolescent playing Professor Higgins rather unconvincingly, but then suddenly and throat-constrictingly responding to adult pain as he sings 'I've grown accustomed to her face'. Then ask yourself, I say, which is worse, offending an adult or damaging a child? If you are sure that you are working to advance the wellbeing of children there can only be one answer. I have found governors very responsive to this.

End piece

This is the last chapter. I hope that I have led you to think again about reasons for building this partnership; suggested some appropriate expectations on which to base it; defined boundaries more clearly; persuaded you that you can recruit more effective governors and keep them; and shown how you can develop the governing body as a strong team and manage the work better. I have also emphasised the part that good communication can play, and delineated a role for governing bodies in the process of school improvement and the traumas of change.

I know there are many exhausting aspects of working with governing bodies which heads feel powerless to change. Those who are already pushing themselves to the limit, as I know many headteachers do today, may well see the range of measures I have suggested as a source of still more pressure. Please let me use these last few lines to say that I am not setting you a massive programme of work. Initially you will have to expend a little precious energy to change some long-established patterns of thought and look critically at many working practices which have become dead and unproductive. I believe that this will be a most profitable investment in better relationships and more effective management, saving time and emotional energy. Much of the stress we hear of comes from fighting against change. Understanding the nature of that change, seeing that it is not reversible, can we not exploit its power for good, working with the grain instead? Local management has put the future of schools into the hands of their governors and headteachers, and you have the opportunity to make that relationship work better for your school. You can do it if you want to enough: it is the children who will be the winners.

Appendix I :
How it all began

This guide shows how school governing bodies came to be part of our schools: the framework is the simplest possible history of state schooling. The role of governing bodies is briefly highlighted with each step along the road. The milestones are Education Acts, and now and then other happenings which have special importance for school governors.

1. State aid: the first public finance for schooling

There was no involvement of public authorities in schooling before 1833, but there were a considerable number of schools scattered around the country. Some were founded by wealthy individuals, some by guilds, some by charities and some by religious orders and the churches. In early Victorian times the only providers of elementary education on any scale were the Anglican and Roman Catholic churches. With the development of industry they found it hard to meet the needs of a growing population increasingly concentrated in towns, so in 1833 Parliament voted to provide a modest grant of £20,000 to help build and maintain both Church of England and Roman Catholic schools. This was the first small gesture of public acceptance of responsibility for basic education, and it was a condition of grant aid that the schools were open to inspection and had local boards of managers (we should now call them governors) to make sure the money was well spent.

> *Accountability* *The belief that public spending on schools should bring with it a combination of national quality control and local management has lasted without serious challenge for well over a hundred years.*

Relationship with church schools The next 40 years saw a big expansion of church schools, which were later to become full partners in state education. This bit of history is essential if you want to understand the special powers and responsibilities which the original providing churches retain to this day in voluntary aided schools. In fact there are very few countries where the choice of a church school is available to parents within the state system, and it is quite remarkable that it should have survived so long through many changes in the structure of public provision.

2. 1870, and the beginnings of a public schooling system

Even with state aid the churches' efforts fell behind the changing needs of the population. The driving force for another big change came from three sources.

1 The churches still immensely valued moral influences in early childhood and literacy, which they saw as the key to the scriptures and a more God-fearing people.
2 The new industrialists needed a better educated workforce.
3 The politicians, following the grant of the vote to all adult males, saw that informed choice required education.

The *Elementary Education Act of 1870* was the result. It aimed to cover the country with schools, and this was to be done by setting up locally elected school boards (the forerunners of our LEAs) wherever there was a shortage. The boards had power to raise local rates to build schools and pay teachers, and the sum raised locally would be matched by a grant from central government. This is still basically how education is funded except that, since 1980–81 (two Local Government Acts in those years), there has been no guarantee that local councils would be able to spend as much as they and their voters thought necessary, never mind have it matched from taxation. (Hence the outcry in recent years against rate-capping.)

Accountability Again all the schools provided under this Act had to be open to inspection and to have a body of local managers to see that everything was done properly at school level.

The School Boards paid the running costs of all the elementary schools, including those provided by the churches. Within 10 years elementary education was made compulsory and within 20 it became free.

3. School governors in Victorian times

So far we have only looked at public elementary schools, and briefly referred to the local boards of managers (as they were called in the state system until 1980) which these schools were required to have. But as stated above there had been for centuries before a great variety of schools, though small in total number, provided by all sorts of agencies. Generally speaking any school, whoever had provided it, would have a board of governors (note the different term) or trustees, local lay people who would oversee its expenditure and ensure that it was well run, and this was seen to be important as far back as the fourteenth century at least. In Victorian times these bodies were to attract some public interest.

> *Accountability It is interesting that the idea of education needing a body of people from outside the school to oversee its work was generally accepted long before there was any taxpayers' money involved or any suggestion of compulsory school attendance. The role of these governors was, as it has in general terms remained, to ensure that the schools were well conducted and to provide accountability to their founders.*

Perhaps people understood that schools affected the quality of everybody's life, whether everybody attended them or not.

Even though these were independently financed schools there was some public interest in how they were governed, and concern to reduce widely differing practice and prevent abuses, and this led to the setting up of two commissions of enquiry into the governance of the public and endowed schools, the Clarendon Commission and the Taunton Commission respectively, round about the middle of the nineteenth century. They sound very modern in the things they emphasise, especially when they talk about the territorial boundaries between the headteacher's work and that of the governors. It was very clearly stated that the 'what' of the curriculum was the governors' responsibility and the 'how' that of the head and staff. Teaching methods and the arrangement of lessons and teaching groups were seen as professional matters, but governors decided on additions to, or deletions from, the range of subjects offered and their content. Typically they would also appoint (and where necessary dismiss) the head, oversee the budget, keep a watch on standards, and ensure that the aims of the founders were honoured.

4. 1902: the consolidation of the public system

The School Board provision was about meeting needs, but the Education Act 1902 was the first measure to impose some neat nationwide framework for schooling and encourage the growth of secondary education. Local Education Authorities were set up with responsibility for both elementary and secondary education, to plan and provide for a wide variety of needs. They also took over responsibility for the curriculum of the church schools, apart from its religious aspects. Secondary schools were provided and maintained by county borough and county councils, while elementary schools were the responsibility of smaller authorities in areas where these existed (often referred to as the Part

Three authorities after the section of the Act concerned). Elementary schools catered up to the compulsory leaving age of 14 and on a voluntary basis to 16. Secondary education was not free, but the county grammar schools offered scholarships to those who passed a selective examination. The new LEAs shared with the churches responsibility for teacher training.

> *Accountability* Again, provision was made for LEAs to delegate local responsibility to bodies of managers and governors, the latter term only used in secondary schools.

A number of large, mainly city, authorities resisted the requirement to have school-level governance, and broke the spirit of the law by appointing combined boards to serve huge numbers of schools, at extremes all the schools in one big city. It took almost a hundred years to end grouping altogether – 1999 in fact.

5. 1944: a dream of life-long entitlement for all

Heightened social awareness The Second World War involved the whole population of this country, civilians as well as armed forces, more than any previous conflict. There had never been such a mixing of social classes. Public school boys worked in the pits while debutantes farmed the land. Men and women with little education from poor homes often found themselves in command of events. People shared rations for christening cakes, borrowed wedding dresses, and everybody unpicked knitted garments to recycle. Travel became a normal activity for many who had never before left their home town. Evacuation took East Enders to stately homes and suburban children to mining valleys. There was the equality of the ration book, the telegram and the grave.

Schooling for a better world Such conditions made people think. When the war was over there was an overwhelming desire to build a better world with education at its heart. The result – reflecting the same feelings and similar in importance to the building of a social security system after the Beveridge Report – was the *Education Act of 1944*, a product of political consensus and long preparation, which was designed to provide an education as broad as it was long for all. It did not fully match these grand words, but it was a brave try. It established primary education and separate free secondary education for all, up to 14 and eventually 16. Secondary schools were to be allocated according to 'age, ability and aptitude' which over much of the country meant selection at 11 for grammar, technical or secondary modern schools. Some privately run schools became direct grant schools with places available for able pupils from LEA primary schools. Pupils unable to benefit from mainstream education were provided for in special schools.

Supplementary services LEAs' duties went beyond the provision of schooling, however. They were required to provide for the 16–19 student, award grants for higher education and teacher training, and provide milk, meals and transport to school. They were empowered to provide nursery education, adult education and provision for recreation and leisure, and to award clothing grants for poor children and maintenance grants for those remaining beyond compulsory school age.

The partnership of church and state This partnership was made legal in a relationship which has lasted with scarcely any change for over 50 years. Church schools could choose whether to become aided or controlled, the former retaining some financial responsibility for the fabric of the building in return for considerable independence, and the latter keeping some protection for their denominational character although all costs were paid by the LEA.

> *Accountability* *All schools had to have a body of local managers in primary schools and governors in secondary schools. (The different names were to last until 1980, when all became governors.) Little guidance was given as to who should be appointed to these bodies, but their powers were set out in model Articles of Government and included:*
>
> - *the general conduct of the school;*
> - *financial supervision;*
> - *sharing in the appointment of the head;*
> - *looking after the premises;*
> - *settling disputes of various kinds.*
>
> *In voluntary schools the boards also had responsibility for maintaining the ethos of the school on behalf of those who provided them.*

6. The years between

No major legislation but a great deal of talking There was not to be another *major* Education Act until 1980, but a great deal was happening, in particular a ferment about secondary education which from the mid-1960s became comprehensive in most areas. There was also a great deal of controversy about primary school methods and a strong backlash in the 1970s (and still with us) against the child-centred style which had developed. Finally, and, for our purposes most important, strong feelings developed about consumers' rights on most things and lively demands for more participation by parents and community in schools.

Action and reaction In wartime and the reconstruction period which followed, everything had been subordinate to the major purpose. In the world of goods and services, value for money, fitness for purpose and fair shares had been paramount, and central direction to achieve these goals was accepted: rationing, the utility scheme, everything plain, fair and worthy. There followed a strong reaction – choice, variety, individualism had a ball for a short time, with a bonfire of controls, burgeoning imports and less rigid social standards. Again a reaction – suddenly fitness for purpose and value for money didn't seem so dull after all, and consumer pressures were to produce an explosion of interest in standards of all kinds and accountability to the consumer in many fields of activity. The role of parents in schools became a talking point and the growing number of parent-teacher associations in schools began to federate. Other organisations representing parents and consumers sprang up in the early 1960s and the National Association of Governors and Managers was formed. The Plowden Report (*Children and their Primary Schools*, HMSO 1967) emphasised the role of home and community in primary schools and was to prove influential.

School governance under the microscope School managers and governors did not escape this debate. The system had gradually fallen into disrepair. Neglect of legal requirements had combined with party political dominance in some areas to damage its place in public esteem. LEAs were by present standards very powerful, and some kept a heavy hand on schools at the expense of the neighbourhood accountability which had been intended. People lost confidence in the ability of this system to prevent creativity in schools degenerating into licence, and when a local school hit the headlines for any reason, the governors often came over as ineffective.

7. The Taylor Committee 1975–77

This Committee was set up by a Labour Government in 1975 to look into the whole question of how schools made their decisions, and in particular to make recommendations on the composition of managing and governing bodies and the respective roles of the LEA, the managers or governors and the headteacher. Its members came from all sections of the education service – LEA members and officers, the churches, colleges of education, headteachers, teachers and parents.

> *The Committee recommended an equal partnership of LEA, elected parents, elected teachers and community in the governing bodies of county (now community) schools, with voluntary schools being reorganised as far as practicable on the same lines. The name 'governors' should be used in both primary and secondary schools. Governing bodies should have a clear strategic role, and such training as was thought necessary should be provided by the LEA. This report was partially implemented in 1980 and almost wholly implemented in 1986.*

8. Children with special needs: the Education Act 1981

Another Education Act in 1981 (following the Warnock Report) radically changed the education of children with disabilities or learning difficulties, who had previously been labelled to indicate the nature of their need. Many of them were in special schools, some in mainstream schools with extra help. Although it was not a major structural act it was very important for the children concerned and their families. Its provisions were largely repeated and extended in the 1993 Act. The 1981 Act said that, as far as possible without damaging their education or that of others, these children were to be educated in future in mainstream schools with such support as they needed. Special schools remained for those for whom integration was impracticable. Children with more serious difficulties (whether or not in special schools) would be given a formal statement of their needs and of the help appropriate. Parents were to be involved in assessments of needs and *governors were made clearly responsible for ensuring that special needs in their schools were properly identified and adequately met.* For a large number of children and parents 1981 was a milestone, and in its time represented very new thinking. It has been described out of date order because the 1980–88 Education Acts were so closely related.

9. The Education Acts of 1980 and 1986 and the reform of governing bodies

The 1980 Act was in some ways just a curtain-raiser. It established parents' rights to express a preference for a school and to have information about schools to help them with that decision: looking back it clearly foreshadowed the more sweeping changes on choice and competition in the 1988 Act.

It also made a gesture towards the Taylor recommendations by establishing minimum representation of parents and teachers on the governing bodies of all schools, but with the LEAs' and churches' representatives still in a majority.

The 1986 Act implemented the Taylor Report almost in full at least as far as county (LEA-provided) schools were concerned.

1 For the first time there were national rules on the total size and composition of governing bodies and their powers.

2 Every school had to have its own governing body, with the sole exception of two neighbouring primary schools which could share a board at the LEA's discretion. Even this pairing was made illegal in 1998.

3 Every county school had to have roughly a quarter of its total number elected by parents and one or two members by teachers. The LEA would

appoint about a quarter and between three and six would be co-opted (by the other governors) from the local community.

4   Voluntary aided schools as before had one elected parent (plus one on the foundation group) and one or two teachers, with a majority of foundation governors over all other groups combined. The arrangements lasted until the 1998 Act, which significantly improved parent representation.

5   These governing bodies had a role in all important decisions of the school – spending, staffing, curriculum, premises and discipline.

6   They had to report annually to parents on their work and arrange a meeting with parents to discuss the report and the running of the school, and had to ensure that parents received a wide range of information about the school's policies and achievements.

10. The Education Reform Act 1988

This is the Act which is seen by professionals as the source of the new and (in many teachers' view) excessive powers of governing bodies. It was an Act which caused widespread misunderstanding, because it linked two quite separate strands of history – one a centuries-old desire to give ordinary people a role in schools, the other a much more recent belief in market forces as a way of improving education. The latter belief was on the whole suspected and feared by those who worked in schools. But it was the 1986 Act which increased participation and the 1988 Act which stressed choice and competition. The extension of the governing body's powers in this later Act merely reflected the extra management responsibilities given to schools, but tended to be seen by teachers as part of an alien policy. Messengers were being blamed for messages they didn't write, and relationships sometimes suffered.

The main aim of the 1988 Act will be seen in time to come as an attempt to give both central government and the school more power at the expense of the local authority, and also to increase competition within the state schooling system. The latter was to be achieved by:

●   increasing choice (for some) by forcing schools to admit up to an agreed capacity – thus restricting LEAs' freedom to protect unpopular schools by catchment areas;

●   introducing key stage testing to measure schools against delivery of a standard product (the national curriculum) and publishing test and exam results to influence parents' choice;

●   through local management, making most of schools' income dependent on numbers recruited, thus still further increasing the impact of parental choice;

●   creating competition within the state system through the establishment of grant-maintained schools (with privileged funding) and city technology colleges;

●   by abolishing the Inner London Education Authority, striking a blow against what the government regarded as excessive protection of unpopular schools and extravagance.

This process – which teachers on the whole disliked – had very little to do with the role of the governing body, but inevitably some of the opposition from heads and teachers rubbed off.

Indeed, many blamed everything they disliked in the package on the reform of governing bodies which happened almost at the same time. Yet most people welcomed the advent the self-managing school, which gave schools so much more flexibility and scope for initiative: few would want to turn the clock back. There is also much support for the national curriculum among teachers, parents and the general public.

To return to the governors' role, the Act provided that the governing body should:

- *share responsibility for the delivery of the national curriculum;*
- *see that religious education and worship were provided as prescribed;*
- *choose the head and deputy;*
- *decide on arrangements for appointing other staff;*
- *set the budget;*
- *be responsible for all personnel matters, including discipline, grievance and pay.*

11. Pressure to raise standards: 1992, 1993, 1997 and 1998

These Acts are considered together, for although they span a change of government their main purpose is to continue the pressure on schools to raise standards and to involve in that process the Office for Standards in Education (OFSTED), LEAs and governing bodies. Perhaps inevitably they put more emphasis on identifying and exposing failure than on nourishing good practice, and this had led to criticism. *The Schools Act 1992* established OFSTED and a regular schedule of school inspections. The inspectors were obliged to consult a general meeting of parents before carrying out the inspection and

the governing body were required to respond to the inspectors' findings by producing an action plan which, like the report itself, was available to all parents. The governing body also had to report regularly to parents on progress in implementing the plan. Later on it was made part of OFSTED inspectors' brief to examine the part played by the governing body in the life of the school and its decisions, and include their findings in the report.

The Education Act 1993 brought about changes in the control of education by establishing the Funding Agency for Schools (FAS – abolished from April

1999) to regulate grant-maintained schools; made it easier to seek GM status; and provided for the FAS to take over the LEA's planning role when local opting out reached a certain level.

The Act made a few changes in the composition of GM schools' governing bodies and laid down some rules for their conduct. It also made truancy an offence in all schools, with parents liable to prosecution, abolished the category of indefinite exclusion and limited short-term exclusions to 15 days' total in any term. LEAs had to set up referral units for pupils out of school, and the balance of excluded pupils' funding had to be transferred to the receiving school.

The provisions of most interest to governors, however, were these:

- governing bodies acquired corporate status which protected their individual members legally and financially;
- arrangements were made for the special measures which would apply to a school found to be failing and its closure if it did not improve;
- social and moral aspects of sex education had to be included in the governing body's sex education provision in all secondary schools (in primary schools the governing body were to decide whether to provide anything beyond the national curriculum science units in their policy);
- the Act repeated the previous provisions on special needs (including governors' responsibility), strengthened SEN children's parents' rights, introduced a new SEN Tribunal to hear appeals and provided for the Secretary of State to issue a Code of Practice.

The Consolidated Education Act 1996 brought together all previous legislation, which would have been very useful – if it had not been followed by further Acts in 1997 and 1998! The Education Act of 1997 continued the school improvement theme by establishing base-line testing for five-year-olds so that published data on school performance could be more fairly compared on a value-added basis. It changed the rules on exclusion by limiting fixed-term exclusions to 45 days in any school year and established governors' responsibility to meet and hear parents' representations after a fixed-term exclusion of more than five days and, as previously, determine the outcome in cases of permanent exclusions. It also required the governing body to draw up home-school agreements setting out the respective expectations of parents and schools, and made their discretionary power to draw up behaviour guidelines a legal requirement.

12. The School Standards and Framework Act 1998

This was enacted by the new Labour government but will surely be seen as part of the same drive towards school improvement, clearer expectations on discipline in schools, and more responsibilities for governors. It provided for:

- *reducing infant class sizes to 30;*
- *LEAs to publish development plans to raise standards;*
- *Education Action Zones to be designated where general standards are low;*
- *a move towards national guidelines and local rules on admissions;*
- *early years development partnerships for under-fives;*
- *(slightly) stronger intervention in failing schools;*
- *parents to ballot on future of selection in existing grammar schools;*
- *nutritional standards for school meals.*

As for governing bodies, they are given clear responsibility for:

- *improving school performance and attendance;*
- *establishing home-school agreements;*
- *drawing up behaviour guidelines;*
- *ensuring the new school meals' nutritional standards;*
- *continuing to decide to confirm or reverse exclusions;*
- *responding to consultations at LEA and school level on a variety of local and school proposals and policies.*

A fuller account of the new powers of governing bodies under this Act is given in Appendix II.

The Act also makes some changes in the constitution of governing bodies. Every school now has its own governing body. Articles (but not Instruments) of Government having been abolished in 1997, much of the detail of governing bodies' powers and procedures is now in the Act itself and its Schedules and the regulations made under it. Nearly all schools have an increase in parent-governor numbers, and voluntary aided schools, as well as having small increases in elected parent representation, must now have enough extra parents among the foundation group to put the total more or less on a par with the number in community schools. The LEA is represented on grant-maintained schools' governing bodies. All schools other than the smallest have a representative of the support staff. There is a little flexibility on size and composition, especially for smaller schools. (Detail in Appendix III.)

13. Summing up

This completes a condensed account of the legal changes which have built our state schooling system over about 150 years. From very simple beginnings it has grown into a vast network of rights, duties and responsibilities, with constant changes in the balance of power between central government, local authority and school. You will see that one of the most constant elements has been the belief that every school needs a body of non-experts to represent the public interest and to keep a watchful eye on the school's healthy development. This has remained at the heart of legislation through very considerable changes in the balance of power between central and local government. More decisions about the individual school are made at school level than ever before. All the signs are that this process will continue, and with it the increase in the importance of governing bodies as the source of strategic policies and as agents of accountability.

Appendix II:
The School Standards and Framework Act 1998 – How it affects schools and governors

The School Standards and Framework Act 1998 is designed to promote school improvement. It redefines and extends the role of school governing bodies, and alters their membership. This brief summary of the Act concentrates on governors' responsibilities but includes details of other changes which will affect their work. (The detail of the new membership of governing bodies is given in Appendix III. Most provisions took effect by September 1999.)

1. Class size

Local education authorities (LEAs) are required to publish plans for ensuring that infant class sizes will not exceed 30 by the year 2000–2001. This will be funded by a grant from the Secretary of State (ss. 1–4).

2. Categories of school

There are to be three main kinds of school in the public system.

1 *Community schools* (mainly former county schools) including community special schools.
2 *Voluntary schools* (both aided and controlled) as before.
3 *Foundation schools* (mainly former grant-maintained schools) including foundation special schools.

Schools falling into category 3 will need to establish, if they don't already have one, a foundation trust to hold the property for the purposes of a school and appoint foundation governors. From April 1999 their funds come from the

LEA; the Funding Agency for Schools (FAS) ceased to exist on that date. Schools may apply to move to a different category, and governors will be involved in these procedures (ss. 20 and 21 and Schedules 2 and 8).

3. Powers and duties of Local Education Authorities

Every LEA must set up a school organisation committee with representatives of the Authority and the relevant Anglican and Roman Catholic Dioceses (s. 24). The LEA must publish a School Organisation Plan, showing how it proposes to meet the needs of the area (s. 26). This must allow for local objections and must be approved by either the school organisation committee or by one of the local adjudicators appointed by the Secretary of State (s. 25, see below). It also has to publish an Education Development Plan for the area, following local consultation, to show how it intends to improve standards (ss. 6 and 7). LEAs have a duty to promote school improvement (s. 4) and have powers to intervene in schools which are not performing well (ss. 14–17). These powers include the appointment of additional governors to schools which have been classed after inspection as failing schools, and the withdrawal of delegated powers from such schools and from schools which have mismanaged their delegated funds. LEAs no longer have powers to reinstate excluded pupils after appeal to governors has failed, but independent tribunals for the purpose will still be established by LEAs in community schools and governors in others (s. 67).

4. New forms of intervention by the Secretary of State

The Secretary of State has new powers to direct *LEAs* who in his/her opinion are not adequately carrying out their functions, and for this purpose must have access to any records of LEAs or schools. The Secretary of State must appoint adjudicators with powers to determine a range of local issues. As before additional governors can be appointed to failing schools and these may in future be paid. He may direct a local authority to close a school judged to need special measures and not sufficiently improved (ss. 8, 18, 19, 25, and 27).

5. Governors' responsibilities

1 *Articles of Government* for individual schools (but not Instruments of Government which will still set out the membership) have been *abolished*, so powers and procedures will in future all be laid down in the law itself or in statutory regulations.

2 As previously, the 1998 Act gives governors responsibility for the *general conduct of the school*, but also adds a responsibility to promote *high standards of performance and attendance*, including target-setting for both (ss. 38 and 63).

3 Governors must also establish a general *complaints procedure* for all matters not covered by statutory complaints provisions elsewhere (s. 39). (Note: implementation was postponed.)

4 The Act confirms their responsibility for the *delegated budget* (s. 49); for *selection of head and deputy and other staff* (this latter can be delegated as the governing body thinks fit, but it remains responsible – detailed staffing procedures are in Schedules 16 and 17); for the *use of the premises outside school hours* (s. 40); and for *setting starting and finishing times for school sessions* (s. 41).

5 On discipline, *the option to lay down guidelines to promote good behaviour becomes a requirement* (s. 61), *and as before governors have power to reinstate a pupil permanently excluded.* If parents make representations even on a fixed-term exclusion exceeding five days or involving missing a public examination the governors must hear them, as well as judging whether to confirm the school's decision in all such cases(ss. 64–66).

6 The governing body continues to share responsibility for ensuring that the *national curriculum* is delivered. It is also responsible for seeing that *religious education and worship* are provided according to the law (but see *Religious Worship* below); for making sure that *special educational needs* are identified and suitably met; and for deciding on the school's *sex education policy*.

7 The requirements to involve governors in general matters (e.g. local reorganisation, closure or change of status of schools) spread across the Act but in general they will have an input into any major decision which affects their school.

8 The Act confirms governors' responsibility for *reporting annually to parents* on their work and arranging an *annual meeting* with parents to discuss the report and any other matters concerning the running of the school (ss. 42 and 43).

9 Governors have a new responsibility for drawing up a *home-school agreement* setting out the aims and values of the school, the responsibilities of parents and the expectation of pupils, and using their best endeavours to obtain parents' signatures. The signing of an agreement may not however be made a condition of being awarded a place at the school (ss. 110 and 111).

10 Finally, all governing bodies will have the same power to buy and sell land or property, accept gifts, enter into contracts, borrow money and invest money as grant-maintained schools had, except that (a) community schools may not enter into contracts of employment with teachers (as foundation and voluntary aided schools may do) and (b) to borrow money or grant security schools need written agreement from the Secretary of State or (if he/she so delegates that power) from the LEA (Schedule 10).

6. Education Action Zones

Where standards of achievement are low over a geographical area, the Secretary of State may designate it an *Education Action Zone* (s. 10). Some have already been named. In such areas various special measures will apply. Among them is a local Education Action Forum to deal with common problems, on which all participating governing bodies may be represented and to which individual schools' powers may in certain circumstances be delegated (s. 12). National provisions on teachers' pay and conditions may be suspended if thought necessary to attract and retain teachers in those areas.

7. Parent-governors on Education Committees

Between two and five elected parent-governors are to be elected to represent parents on the Education Committee in every LEA from June 2000 (s. 9).

8. Religious worship

Every pupil in a maintained school must take part in an act of worship every day (s. 70). The Act no longer requires that this takes place for the whole school at one time. This interpretation is spelled out in Schedule 20, which also makes it clear that in community or non-religious foundation schools it shall be of a broadly Christian character on a majority of occasions in any one term.

9. Nursery education

Every LEA will have a duty to provide sufficient education, either at school or elsewhere, suitable for children under compulsory school age. To support this duty they must establish in every LEA an early years development partnership, and in consultation with its members prepare an early years development plan for the approval of the Secretary of State. Children under school age with special educational needs must be provided for in accordance with the Code of Practice established under s. 313 of the Education Act 1996. Assistance with travel costs may be provided for children receiving nursery education otherwise than at school. All nursery provision provided by LEAs or grant assisted will be inspected by qualified and registered nursery education inspectors from a register maintained by Her Majesty's Chief Inspectors (ss. 117–124 and Schedule 26).

10. School meals

There will once more be established nutritional standards for school meals where these are provided, and responsibility for providing meals and complying with the standards will be transferred to the governing body where they are currently provided by the LEA (ss. 114–116).

11. Constitution of governing bodies

There will be some changes in size and membership of all governing bodies (*see* Appendix III for details).The main changes are the abolition of shared governing bodies (previously allowed for two close primary schools), improved parent representation in almost all schools, LEA representation in former grant-maintained (now foundation) schools, and a support staff-governor in all but the very smallest schools (where it is optional). There is also some flexibility for schools themselves, particularly small schools, and regulations will provide for extra co-options in certain circumstances.

Appendix III :
Structure of governing bodies

The following structure has been operative since September 1999.

General Every school must have a separate governing body – no more grouping of primary schools as allowed under the 1980 Act and subsequently. In all schools the headteacher is a governor unless at any time he/she decides otherwise (previously GM heads had no choice of opting out of being a governor). In all primary schools where there is a minor authority one co-opted place must go to a representative of that authority. If there are more than one the governors decide which.

Primary and special schools

A *Community Primary School* 4 or 5 parent-governors, 3 or 4 LEA governors, 1 or 2 teacher-governors, 1 staff-governor, 3 or 4 co-opted governors.

B *Community Primary School under 100 pupils* This is an option – governors to choose between A and B. 3 parent-governors, 2-LEA governors, 1 teacher-governor, 1 or 0 staff-governor, 2 co-opted governors.

C *Community Special School* May choose between A and B regardless of size. 1 co-opted governor shall be replaced in a hospital school by a representative of the Health Authority or Trust and in any other school by a representative of appropriate voluntary organisation(s).

D *Foundation Primary School* 5 or 6 parent-governors, 2 LEA governors, 1 teacher-governor, 1 staff-governor, 3 or 4 foundation governors, 1 co-opted governor.

E *Foundation Primary School under 100 pupils* May choose between D and E. 4 parent-governors, 2 LEA governors, 1 teacher-governor, 1 or 0 staff-governor, 2 foundation governors, 1 co-opted governor.

F *Voluntary Controlled Primary School* 4 or 5 parent-governors, 3 LEA governors, 1 teacher-governor, 1 staff-governor, 3 or 4 foundation governors, 1 co-opted governor.

G *Voluntary Controlled Primary School under 100 pupils* May choose between F and G. 3 parent-governors, 2 LEA governors, 1 teacher-governor, 1 or 0 staff-governor, 2 foundation governors, 1 co-opted governor.

H *Voluntary Aided Primary School* 1 or 2 parent-governors, 1 or 2 LEA governors, 1 teacher-governor, 1 staff-governor, sufficient foundation governors to give a majority of two overall, and two of these at least must be parents.

I *Voluntary Aided Primary School under 100 pupils* May choose between H and I. 1 parent-governor, 1 LEA governor, 1 teacher-governor, 1 or 0 staff-governor, foundation governors as in H.

Secondary schools

J *Community Secondary School* 6 parent-governors, 5 LEA governors, 2 teacher-governors, 1 staff-governor, 5 co-opted governors.

K *Community Secondary School under 600 pupils* May choose between J and K. 5 parent-governors, 4 LEA governors, 2 teacher-governors, 1 staff-governor, 4 co-opted governors.

L *Foundation Secondary School* 7 parent governors, 2 LEA governors, 2 teacher-governors, 1 staff-governor, 4 foundation governors, 2 co-opted governors.

M *Foundation Secondary School under 600 pupils* May choose between L and M. 6 parent-governors, 2 LEA governors, 2 teacher-governors, 1 staff-governor, 4 foundation governors, 2 co-opted governors.

N *Voluntary Controlled Secondary School* 6 parent governors, 2 LEA governors, 2 teacher-governors, 1 staff-governor, 5 foundation governors, 2 co-opted governors.

O *Voluntary Controlled Secondary School under 600 pupils* May choose between O and N. 5 parent-governors, 3 LEA governors, 2 teacher-governors, 1 staff-governor, 4 foundation governors, 2 co-opted governors.

P *Voluntary Aided Secondary School* 3 parent-governors, 2 LEA governors, 2 teacher-governors, 1 staff-governor, sufficient foundation governors to give an overall majority of 3. Three of these must be parents.

Q *Voluntary Aided Secondary School under 600 pupils* may choose between P and Q. 2 parent-governors, 1 LEA governor, 2 teacher-governors, 1 staff-governor, sufficient foundation governors to give an overall majority of 2. Two of these must be parents.

Where in any category there is a choice of numbers for more than one kind of governor, e.g. in voluntary aided primary schools one or two parent governors and one or two LEA governors, a governing body must choose the higher or lower option wholesale, i.e. no mixing and matching.

Appendix IV:

Working together rules

These guidelines incorporate the regulations made under the Education Standards and Framework Act 1998 (SI 1999/2163) which took effect on 1 September 1999. Small amendments were made to take effect in September 2000 and these are included where appropriate. The regulations have the force of law. They exist to protect the vital corporate power of the governing body and prevent individuals or groups from becoming too powerful. They are based on every governor's equal right to contribute, the only exception being when a particular governor has a conflict of interest. They ensure that important decisions are made only when enough governors are present, that governors have the information they need about the meeting and the business to be transacted, and that governing bodies make decisions thoughtfully. They set out sensible procedures to ensure fair and purposeful discussion. Please remember all these points when you are tempted to see rules as dull and bureaucratic. They protect governors' rights, and every head and governor should know them. The numbers of the appropriate regulation are shown in brackets.

1. Meetings Governors must meet at least once a term: most will need to meet more often. Seven days' notice is required, with the Agenda and relevant papers (34). At the first meeting of the school year the governing body must elect a Chair and Vice-Chair: neither of these can be a person employed at the school (29). A contested election must be held by secret ballot (29(10)). If possible, nominations for chair should be made in writing with the agenda (29(11)(c)). A quorum of two-thirds of governors in post (i.e. not counting vacancies) is required for this election (September 2000 amendment). If there are no nominations names can be put forward at the meeting (29(11)(d)). Governors must also at least once a year review their committee arrangements – elect members and agree terms of reference and method of working (46(b)). The Chair may call a special meeting without the usual period of notice if necessary (34(5)(b)), and if any three governors request a special meeting, the clerk must arrange it as soon as possible (34(4)).

2. Clerk The clerk has to be chosen by the governing body. This office cannot now be held by a serving governor. A clerk can be dismissed by a decision of the whole governing body (22, 23 and 24).

3. How decisions are made The governing body's responsibilities are corporate: the only legal decisions are those made together at properly convened meetings or delegated within the regulations. Governors as individuals have no power, except in an emergency, the Chair (see *Powers of the Chair* below). Decisions are made after discussion by general agreement or majority vote. The Chair has a second or casting vote if votes for and against are equal. In some circumstances a governor may not be able to play a part in making a decision because of conflict of interest (see *Conflict of interest* below).

4. The headteacher is a full member of the governing body unless he/she decides otherwise. The head may attend all meetings of the governing body and its committees (32), except when they relate to the appointment of his/her successor (September 2000 amendment) or where there is a conflict of interest, e.g. when a decision is being made on an excluded pupil. This applies whether or not the head chooses to be a governor.

5. Powers of the Chair The Chair provides leadership for the governing body but has no powers to act on their behalf without instructions except in an emergency, and even then only if the action is one which may legally be delegated (see *Delegating functions* below). An emergency is defined as a situation which threatens the well-being of the school or any pupil, parent or staff member and where there is no time to call a special meeting (43). The governing body has power to remove the Chair from office if there is widespread dissatisfaction among them: the detailed procedures are rigorous (e.g. they spread over two meetings, there is full provision for reasons to be given and replied to and the higher level of quorum applies) (30). The power to remove the Chair does not apply to a Chair appointed by the DfEE to a school in special measures, who can only be removed by the Department (September 2000 amendment). If the Chair resigns or is removed mid-term, there must be an election: the Vice-Chair does not automatically inherit (29(6)). No employee of the school may chair the governing body (29(5)(b)) or one of its statutory committees (see Para. 9).

6. Quorum To make a legal decision a certain proportion of governors must be present. For most matters this is one-third of the total membership (including vacancies) but for certain decisions a higher quorum of two-thirds of governors in post and eligible to vote is required (37). The main decisions requiring a higher quorum relate to co-opting or otherwise appointing a governor, electing or removing the Chair, and delegating functions. Note that there is a different method of calculating the quorum in the two cases, the normal one being calculated from a total which includes vacancies and governors ineligible to vote, the larger one including only governors in post and eligible to vote, so less stringent.

7. Non-attendance A governor who, without the permission of the governing body, has not attended a meeting for six months, is automatically disqualified (Schedule 5 (4) (2)). If it is an LEA or representative governor, a foundation governor or a co-opted governor, he/she may not be reappointed to the same governing body in that capacity for 12 months (Schedule 5 (4) (5)). In order to make disqualification mean something, governors must always record, when a member apologises for absence, that they accept the apology and the reasons. Otherwise it does not count.

8. Delegating functions Governors are allowed to delegate some functions to individuals or committees, but there are many exceptions which are given in full in your Guide to the Law (41). Among those which *cannot* be delegated are:

> *(a) alteration, closure or change of character of school;*
>
> *(b) appointment of chair and vice-chair;*
>
> *(c) forming committees and delegating functions;*
>
> *(d) submitting the budget to the LEA each year;*
>
> *(e) co-opting, appointing, or removing governors;*
>
> *(f) ratifying choice of new head or deputy;*
>
> *(g) arranging appeals against dismissal;*
>
> *(h) policies on admission, school discipline, collective worship, sex education, charging for activities, fixing school terms, holidays and times of sessions;*
>
> *(i) delegating functions to an Education Action Forum or requesting their reinstatement;*
>
> *(j) agreeing the annual report to parents, the prospectus and the home-school agreement.*

9. Committees Governors are required to set up a committee of at least three members (but see note) for staff discipline and one of five members for pupil exclusions and, in voluntary aided schools, one for admissions (47, 48 and 49) these are called statutory committees. They may set up such other committees as they think fit. For staff discipline they also need a second committee to consider any appeal, and this must exclude governors on the first committee or any others with prior knowledge. Any appeal committee must have no fewer members than the committee which made the decision (47(2)). Note: exceptionally, in very small schools where there are fewer than six governors eligible, the governing body may appoint discipline and appeal committees of two, subject to the second committee always having no fewer members than the first (47(6)). In these cases, however, no decisions can be made unless both members are present (September 2000 amendments).

Non-governors may be co-opted to committees with the governing body's agreement in each individual case, but governors must always be in a majority when voting and only governors may chair a committee: the governing body decides whether these co-opted members have a vote (46(2)(c, d, e, f and h)). No employee of the school may chair a committee with delegated power.

Every committee must be clerked, but in committees other than the statutory committees referred to above (i.e. staff and pupil discipline) the clerk may be appointed by the committee (September 2000 amendments) and can be a member of the governing body (51(1) and (3)). (In the statutory committees the clerk may not be a governor and has to be appointed by the governing body.) Committees must always record their decisions and report to the full governing body (44 and 54).

Governors employed at the school may be involved in discussion of *policies* on pay and staff appraisal, but not in any discussion of the pay or appraisal of an individual.

10. Changing your minds If at any meeting a governing body rescinds a resolution made at a previous meeting, the item must have been on the published agenda for the second meeting as a specific item. If it has not been on the agenda circulated beforehand no decision to reverse the initial decision is legal (35).

11. Co-options Co-opted governors may not vote in future co-options. Since September 1999 staff of the school who are eligible for election as teacher or staff governors have not been eligible to become co-opted governors (Schedule 5 (12)).

12. Removal of governors There are new provisions allowing some types of governor to be removed if this is the wish of a majority of colleagues. Elected (i.e. parent and teacher) governors cannot be removed at all, and LEA and foundation governors can only be removed (for sufficient reason) by the body they represent. Co-opted governors can, however, be removed by resolution of the governing body to which they were co-opted or, in the case of additional co-opted sponsorship governors, on the recommendation of the appointing body (in this case the removal must, however, also have the support of the governing body). The procedure has to be spread over two meetings, with at least 14 days between. In each case the removal must be clearly included on the agenda as an item of business and a resolution must be passed. The governor or governors proposing the removal must give reasons, and the governor concerned must be given an opportunity to respond. If then a resolution to remove is confirmed, the person ceases to be a governor (18(4) and 19). The higher quorum applies. Exactly the same procedure applies to the removal from office (but not in this case from the governing body) of the Chair, if there is widespread dissatisfaction among colleagues with his/her performance (30).

13. Conflict of interest A governor may play no part in a discussion, or vote, if he/she has a pecuniary interest in the outcome, a conflict of interest, or there are circumstances which raise reasonable doubt about his/her ability to be impartial (Schedule 6). (Anyone who is in a position to give evidence on a matter under discussion, e.g. a witness to a disciplinary incident, may, however, be heard by the relevant committee, but if the circumstances are such that that person could not be impartial (e.g. in the case of a pupil excluded for violent behaviour, the parents of a victim) he/she takes no part in the decision. By the same token, although the headteacher would probably present the school's case beforehand in an exclusion case, he/she would withdraw while the decision is made.) It is made clear that a teacher or support staff governor need only withdraw because of a personal interest if that interest is greater than the generality of teachers or support staff (as the case may be) in the school (Schedule 6(5) and (6)). They may not, however, take part in any discussion of the pay or appraisal of a named colleague (Schedule 6(4)) though they may serve on the relevant committees. A new provision in the September 2000 amendments makes it clear that a member of the school staff cannot be present at any meeting about the appointment of his or her successor; previously there had been some queries about whether an out-going head could participate in selecting a successor, and although it seemed to many to be clearly implied in a provision in the main 1998 Act that he/she could not, it was never explicit.

14. Confidentiality, governors' papers and visitors to meetings Observers may attend governors' meetings for any non-confidential business if the governing body so decides (33). They may attend committees if the relevant committee so decides (56(4)). Governors' agenda and papers, and minutes once the Chair has approved them, must be available for any interested party to see, with any confidential items excluded (40). Only the governing body may decide to classify an item as confidential (40(2)). (Classification is intended primarily to protect the privacy of individuals, and it is clearly intended that it should not be used excessively. Governors may disclose non-confidential decisions – but it is vital that they do so accurately and discreetly. It is not good practice to reveal the detail of what individuals said or how they voted, or in any way to be disloyal to colleagues or put the governing body in a bad light.)

> *General comments It cannot be emphasised too strongly that these are not rules for the sake of rules. If you look at them carefully you will see that they are all designed to protect the work governors do together and their individual rights to contribute. They prevent power drifting into too few hands and also protect the work against a governor who may have an axe to grind in a particular item. They make sure that governors take their power seriously and do not give it away lightly. In short, the rules safeguard democratic practice. If all are not equally familiar with them, or they are not taken seriously, it opens the door to abuse of power at best and at worst illegal decisions which could be challenged in a damaging way by aggrieved individuals, by the courts, by local authorities or the Secretary of State.*

Index

■ ■ ■